Blood and *Splendor*

Blood and *Splendor*

THE LIVES OF FIVE TYRANTS, FROM NERO TO SADDAM HUSSEIN

DANIEL MYERSON

Perennial
An Imprint of HarperCollins*Publishers*

Brief excerpts from "The Bacchae" in *Complete Greek Tragedies: Euripides,* ed. David Grene and Richmond Lattimore, University of Chicago Press, 1992.

HarperCollins books may be purchased for educational, business, or sales promotional use. For information please write: Special Markets Department, HarperCollins Publishers Inc., 10 East 53rd Street, New York, NY 10022.

FIRST EDITION

Designed by Philip Mazzone

Library of Congress Cataloging-in-Publication Data is available.

ISBN 0-380-80489-1

01 02 03 04 05 ❖/RRD 10 9 8 7 6 5 4 3 2 1

To Emanuel L. Wolf, history buff, insightful man of a thousand tales, producer of genius, wonderful critic, and kind friend

Walk up! Walk up and spend a pleasant hour,
Ladies who take joy in life, proud gentlemen with me!
Inside my tent you'll thrill and chill to see
The beasts I have in my menagerie . . .

—Alban Berg, *Lulu*

CONTENTS

CONTENTS

ACKNOWLEDGMENTS

Many thanks to Krista Stroever who has inherited this book with grace and enthusiasm and who will, I intuit, contribute greatly to its reception.

I also wish to thank Stephen S. Power for his many chastening suggestions, and above all for his enthusiasm.

Blood and Splendor was the brainchild of Noah Lukeman, literary tyrant par excellence, who conceived it while I was talking to him one day about Ivan the Terrible (with whom I suspect he identifies).

Thanks to Dr. Brenda Shoshanna for providing spiritual insight and to Dr. Leah Kohn for providing psychological perspective. Thanks to Dr. Vivian Heller for helping me track down obscure and racy information. Thanks to Constance and John Skedgell and Mark Roberts for keeping me going. Thanks to Martin Cohen for his many insightful talks on what it means to be a writer. Thanks to Fran Plavé for honest criticism and intense interest. Thanks for the title to Maura Spiegal, a tyrant-manqué if ever there was one. Thanks to Rochelle Gurstein for not having thought of it first. And special thanks to Rabbi Eli Silberstein for information about Stalin.

NERO

I.   A CRIME AND A STAGE DEBUT

You do not know the life you are living. You do not even know your name.
> —A warning given by Dionysus, god of wine, drunkenness, and theater, in Euripides' *The Bacchae*

THE YEAR A.D. 59. ROME. Since the day before, when heralds proclaimed a triumph, one question has been on everyone's lips: Where have the troops won a victory? The question has not yet been answered, though the young emperor, crowned with a victor's laurels, is about to enter the city.

Could there have been a battle with Parthia? After all, Rome's great rival to the east has been defeated but is still independent. Or maybe there has been a rising in Britain? The island-kingdom, conquered not more than twenty years earlier by Nero's predecessor Claudius, has been restless under the Roman yoke. Or perhaps Spain? Germany?

But no one guesses the monstrous truth. Although Romans have become used to the crimes of their emperors, Nero has gone beyond the debauchery of Tiberius and even the madness of Caligula. The streets are hung with tapestries and strewn with flowers, the priests offer up sacrifices, and the people have gathered—to celebrate Nero's murder of his own mother.

Nor does anyone care when the truth becomes known—Spain or Gaul or the emperor's mother, what's the difference? The spectacle is what counts, and no one knows better how to create such dazzling displays than Nero, who bankrupts the treasury with so many festivals that the Senate asks him to leave a few days for work, a request the emperor shrugs off, more interested in pleasing the common people, whom the Senate dismisses as "rabble."

Rabble or not, Nero woos them with gladiatorial shows and feasts and fantastic lotteries. A wooden ball hurled through the air can turn the slave who catches it into an estate-owning aristocrat, thus emphasizing the arbitrary nature of the social order. Then there are the bacchanals, to which the entire city is invited—everyone, that is, except the aristocrats, whom Nero snubs, despising their traditional Roman ways. In their place, actors and charioteers and poets and acrobats sit at his table. Or if the nobility are invited, it is not because the emperor wants to discuss state affairs with them, as was formerly the practice at these *convivias*. Nero asks them to the palace to degrade them, to have their slaves abuse them sexually in public, to seat their wives next to whores, and to give their daughters as prizes to victorious gladiators.

The impulse behind such acts is not simply a perverse one, a flaunting of godlike power, as it was with Caligula. It is that Nero is in his way a revolutionary. He represents something new and subversive on the Roman scene: an emperor playing artist or an artist playing emperor, it is difficult to say which. Indifferent to military glory, Nero devotes himself instead to singing, painting, writing, and acting, not only as a source of private pleasure but for the purpose of launching his career as a public performer. His remark "If I am deposed as emperor, I can always earn my bread as a singer in Alexandria" is not an ironic quip but a daydream—for he is disillusioned with absolute power. Being master of the civilized world bores him. The traditional Roman aristocrats bore him; Nero scorns them as philistines and turns to his Greek subjects for understanding.

For if the Roman genius shows itself in government and world conquest, the Greek spirit finds its fullest expression in art, drama, philosophy, in a spontaneity of consciousness that ill accords with Roman severity and *gravitas* ("dignity"). And it is the Greek spirit that inspires Nero.

Which is the real scandal of his reign—that he values an artist's glory more highly than an emperor's; that he rejects Roman duty for Greek ecstasy; that he prefers the life of imagination to politics and statecraft. When he fantasizes about being a professional singer, it is Alexandria he dreams of, a sophisticated city more Greek than Egyptian, not martial Rome. And although the aristocrats can forgive him his matricide, they cannot forgive him his music.

Whatever the faults of other emperors—Tiberius, for example, who retired to Capri to spend his days in debauchery, or the megalomaniac Caligula, self-indulged to the point of self-apotheosis—they did not challenge the order of the Roman world. But Nero, who will beg on bended knee for the judge's leniency in singing competitions, violates Rome's sense of what an emperor should be. His absolute devotion to his art just adds to the scandal—his hours of practice and study, the massage and special diets to improve his voice, the endless consultations with professional singers. He lies for hours with heavy lead sheets on his chest to strengthen his diaphragm for singing, and practices his harp as he receives senators or other officials who have come to discuss affairs of state.

Even to us, two thousand years later, the disgust of the great Roman historians Suetonius and Tacitus is palpable when they describe Nero's grand performances, the first of which takes place after his mother's death. It is a memorable occasion in Rome's long history. When Agrippina was alive, she kept her son within bounds; if he sang or acted it was only in the palace and only for select friends. But now that she is dead, Nero has decided to celebrate his triumph with his artistic debut. The procession will wind its way through the cheering crowds to the Circus Maximus, where he plans to perform for all his subjects, commoner and aristocrat alike, since not even the disapproving nobility can afford to be absent. That would bring down charges of treason on their heads.

For the masses, though, there is no question of coercion. They are delighted by the news and since early morning have thronged the streets and balconies and rooftops waiting for their emperor to enter the city. There may be talk of the strangeness of this triumph, there may be all kinds of speculation and gossip, but when Nero finally appears at the gates, all questions fall away. A great cry goes up from thousands of throats: *Ave Caesar! Hail!* All Rome gazes with rapture at its hero. *Ave Nero Caesar!*

Robed in purple and gold, he is tall, fleshy, strong, bull-necked, athletic, his expression at once sensitive and dissolute. His ivory chariot is drawn through the city gates by naked slave girls, and he stretches out his arms to his people as lottery balls and a shower of gold coins are tossed left and right. At every step of the way, the people cry out with an admiration that will last long after Nero's reign is finished and he is dead. *No! Not dead. Just in hiding,* the legend will claim, so unwilling are the masses to part with their golden-throated artist-ruler.

Their love for him, however, is a measure of his vulnerability, for it is precisely what the "rabble" adores about Nero that makes him suspect to the army and the praetorian guard, that elite corps dedicated to the emperor. His behavior forces the guards to consider that line between the two roles they played in the past, protectors and assassins, most recently when they claimed a part in the murder of the emperor Caligula and then in the elevation of his uncle Claudius to the throne (whom they found hiding behind the palace curtains and hoisted onto their shoulders, proclaiming the trembling scholar emperor in a wild, spontaneous gesture).

Such is the Roman law of succession—which is to say there is none, for *in theory* the emperor's position is not hereditary. In theory, the Senate has bestowed extraordinary powers upon him, to be exercised only during his lifetime. The idea is that as leader of the nation, the emperor will prevent civil wars of the kind that plagued Rome during the last days of the Republic. In practice, though, the Julian house has become an imperial dynasty, with the emperor naming his own successor and the army and guards confirming his choice. By the time of Nero, the praetorian guards have become more and more important as players in this imperial dice game, and the Senate has been reduced to mere spectatorship. Rome has become what Bismarck would later ironically call Russia: an autocracy tempered by assassination.

Nero understands this well, murder being part of his family heritage, and accordingly he takes every precaution he can, from tasters who sample every dish he is served to spies who fan out through the city to listen for the slightest rumor of conspiracy.

But even so, fear still distorts the emperor's features as he makes his way through his adoring subjects: there is no precaution he can take against his mother's ghost, as she always had protected herself against hostile spirits, and other enemies. He looks out over the city that is now his—that she won for him with her schemes and crimes—and must feel that even death might be unable to stop her, less woman and mother than force of nature, ruthless and relentless, undeterred by human or divine law.

Nero's earliest memory is of being torn out of her arms, not to see his young, beautiful mother again for two years, each year an eternity, measured by the standards of childhood.

Where has she gone? Nero is too young to understand that she has been sent into exile by the emperor Caligula, her brother, who accuses her of treason. Her crime, though, is sexual, not political. Agrippina has slept with one of her brother's male lovers, a young man whom Caligula then has murdered and whose ashes he forces Agrippina to carry away with her to the barren island where she will spend her exile. If the punishment seems harsh, that is because it is a case of double jealousy: Caligula is also his sister's lover, having seduced Agrippina when she was only a girl of twelve and he a boy of fifteen. At that time, the emperor Tiberius married her off to prevent a scandal; Agrippina was given as child bride to Ahenobarbus, a brutal, debauched nobleman who died soon after his only child, Nero, was born.

And so Nero is left without a mother or father. His inheritance stolen, he is raised like a pauper by an indifferent aunt, his father's sister, who begrudges him the barest necessities and entrusts him to the care of two slaves on a country estate in the south. A traveler passing through Calabria during that time would have seen a strange sight: a dark, graceful dancer performing for a dirty-faced urchin who sits on the lap of a potbellied man. An African dancer past her prime, an old, palsied barber, a family of circumstance, ill and mean.

Meanwhile, Agrippina languishes on her gloomy pile of rocks in the middle of the sea, her exile made worse by the fact that a generation before, her mother, Agrippina the Elder, starved herself to death in despair on this same island.★ Each boat that comes near makes Nero's mother tremble, because it might bring a death sentence from her brother. Each shooting star or lightning-blasted tree seems to her a portent of her death. Then, the unexpected: Caligula is stabbed to death by his guards in an underground passage leading to the Circus, and her uncle Claudius, now emperor, recalls his favorite niece to Rome.

Although the doddering Claudius is married to a young and beautiful wife, Messalina, and although he has two children by her, Agrippina is determined to become her uncle's wife and push aside his son for her own. The close blood relation between her and her uncle does not matter to her; in fact, the family lines of the imperial

---

★Agrippina the Elder nursed an implacable hatred of the emperor Tiberius, who out of jealousy had poisoned her much-beloved husband, Germanicus. Tiberius banished her together with her two elder sons, and they all died in exile. Her three remaining daughters and a younger son survived the reign of Tiberius: Nero's mother, Agrippina the Younger, was one of the daughters, and the son was to become the emperor Caligula—who slept with all three of his sisters both before and after his elevation to the throne.

family are so interwoven that Agrippina is *at the same time* aunt and niece to Messalina, whose mother is Domitia Lepida, the frugal aunt who raised Nero. Agrippina makes up her mind that one day Nero will replace Claudius on the throne—why else has she survived her exile? The gods, if they exist, have brought her back to Rome for this purpose. And if they don't exist, so much the better.

Carefully, she insinuates herself into the imperial household, winning over the emperor's guards and servants with bribes and favors. But there is no deceiving Messalina; the two women have taken each other's measure and understand each other. The stakes are high, an empire stretching from the Atlantic to the Caucasus, from Britain to the deserts of Africa.

Messalina makes the first move. Wanting no one to rival her son Britannicus' claims to the throne, she sends slaves to murder Nero while he sleeps. But they are caught before they can harm the boy, a piece of luck ascribed to a snakeskin charm wound around Nero's bed (in later years he will have it set in gold and made into a bracelet which he will wear continually). Agrippina responds by biding her time. She knows that Messalina has a fatal flaw: uncontrollable lust. Although Agrippina has quite a sexual repertoire of her own, ranging from incest to adultery, her motives are not pleasure but power. She always acts with a discretion born of calculation, coldly using her beauty to manipulate her lovers or to win protection.

Messalina is just the opposite; unable to exercise the slightest restraint, she is driven by her sexual appetites to acts that are as dangerous as they are unnatural. Making matters worse is the fact that her husband, Claudius, is a worn-out, jaded glutton and drunkard twice her age, who suffers from a host of physical infirmities and is more interested in his antiquarian studies than in his young wife.

So Agrippina understands that all she must do to win is simply to survive; it is just a matter of time before Messalina destroys herself with her passions, which become more excessive every day. She is insatiable. Her lovers include the young and the old, the handsome and the ugly, sailors, senators, slaves, soldiers, and schoolboys. Even the homosexual actor Mnester is recruited for the empress's pleasure. Later, at his trial, Mnester will almost escape by showing the marks of the whipping Messalina had given him to force him into her bed, but Claudius will decide it is not fitting to spare the life of an actor when so many aristocrats are executed. Collecting regular fees, Messalina prostitutes herself to add piquancy to her indulgence, and finally she decides to marry one of her lovers during an orgy—while she is still married to Claudius. As the wedding ceremony is taking place, however, a loyal freedman informs the emperor, who for the first time learns what everyone else in Rome already knows, that Messalina has turned the palace into a brothel.

It is usually difficult to arouse Claudius to anger. A scholar by temperament, he is good-natured enough not to mind all kinds of jests at his expense. Guests at his banquets throw olive pits at him when he passes out in a drunken stupor, and even his slaves sometimes awaken the emperor with a poke in his ribs. Still, when aroused his anger can be savage. He orders his wife and her lovers arrested en masse and in a series of scandalous trials condemns all of them to death, ordering Messalina to commit suicide, as befits a Roman noblewoman. When the moment comes, she is terrified and has to be helped by her mother, Domitia Lepida.

Agrippina is waiting in the wings with her son. Rome, disgusted by Messalina's profligacy, wants an empress who possesses all the virtues of a Roman matron, and Agrippina knows how to play that part. She marries Claudius and sets about preparing her son for the role of successor. Having grown to a healthy and robust youth who displays his strength and skill at athletic games, Nero also has a prodigious memory and a love for Greek learning and art. Agrippina appoints the Stoic philosopher Seneca to be tutor to her son, instructing him to discourage Nero's artistic pursuits and train him in matters more fitting for a future emperor.

The truth is, Seneca will be an excellent choice. From Seneca, Nero learns the art of speech-making and is taught exactly how to win favor with the public. His first speeches to the Senate are received with great enthusiasm. Though they are actually composed by Seneca, Nero delivers them with so much theatrical flair that he makes a brilliant impression. Britannicus, Claudius' son by Messalina, suffers in comparison. Saddened by his mother's death and afflicted with epilepsy, he is shy and sensitive and awkward in public. His closest companion is his sister, Octavia, whom Agrippina marries off to Nero although the girl is barely nine, because the marriage strengthens her son's claim to the throne.

The marriage is a prelude to Claudius' adoption of Nero and finally, a triumph for Agrippina, the naming of her son as heir in place of his own son, a step which the old emperor doesn't realize is his death warrant. From that moment on, Agrippina watches for the right moment to kill her husband and put her son on his throne.

It is to be a death by poison, but the question is which one? A quick-acting potion would be too obvious, and anything too slow might be dangerous: a man suffering a drawn-out death agony might change his mind, so Claudius must not be allowed to linger too long, either. She calls in a consultant, a woman named Locusta, who

has been sentenced to death for a poisoning. Given a re-
prieve by Agrippina, who is eager to learn her secrets, Locusta produces something subtle that is guaranteed both to
confuse Claudius' faculties and to produce a delayed effect.
Within forty-eight hours, she promises Agrippina, the emperor will be dead. (Locusta will go on to lend a hand in
more than one imperial murder over the next decade before finally being beheaded during the reign of Galba.)

A plate of mushrooms is presented to Claudius during
a banquet, and the taster, in Agrippina's pay, samples the
smaller mushrooms as agreed. Agrippina herself partakes of
the dish, then passes one of the large, succulent, poisoned
mushrooms to her husband and waits for the results with
bated breath. But although he is seized with terrible stomach cramps, a sudden evacuation of the bowels saves him,
and he passes through the crisis unscathed.

Feigning desperation, Agrippina sends for his physician
Xenophon, as though to make sure that Claudius is out of
danger. The learned Greek is also in her pay, however, and
knows what he must do as Agrippina passes him a vial with
another of Locusta's poisons. Dipping a feather into the
lethal mixture, he tickles Claudius' throat to help him
vomit. Again and again he dips the feather into the poison,
until Claudius breaks into a sweat. Shivering, his large body
bloated by gluttony and days of drinking, the emperor falls
into a faint and is carried away to Agrippina's chamber,
where she can "nurse" her husband. By morning he is dead.

In a fever of her own, Agrippina sends messages and
gifts to reassure herself of the loyalty of the palace guard
and to make sure of key officers in the army. Then she
staggers out of the death chamber and hugs Britannicus to
her with tears and lamentations. His resemblance to his father both pierces her with grief and consoles her; she
weeps, she reaches out for Octavia, who flees her embrace

with loathing. It is no matter—Octavia is Nero's wife now, whether she likes it or not, and will play her part.

Turning from the "poor orphans," Agrippina now leads her beloved Nero to the barracks of the guards, who despite encouragement from their officers hear the news of Claudius' death with confusion. An ominous murmur is heard: Where is Britannicus? But then Agrippina steps forward and addresses the soldiers "As the wife of their late emperor Claudius and the daughter of the hero Germanicus." Taking Nero by the hand, she presents him to "her" guards, repeating the will of Claudius, who proclaimed her son heir. The tide is turned. Amidst cheers and an outpouring of enthusiasm the guards greet their new emperor, who is led to the Senate for formal confirmation. There Nero recites a speech prepared by his tutor, a masterpiece of rhetoric that causes Rome to sigh with relief. An auspicious beginning! Nero will rule in the best traditions of the Republic, he promises.

But it is all show. Already Agrippina is preparing a list of enemies she wants out of the way. For she will rule the ruler. Why else did she toil and scheme for so many years? Why else did she put up with Claudius' loathsome embraces? Why else did she murder the old man? If Nero's features are on the coins, hers are next to his—to the right, a sign of greater power. When senators and foreign ambassadors come to seek an audience with the new emperor, the one who will have the last word sits listening behind a curtain near the throne—Agrippina.

She keeps her son close to her, cloaking her crimes in the appearance of strict propriety. The young ruler lives a solitary life under his mother's watchful eye, obeying her orders and remaining an enigma to his subjects, who know him mainly through the virtuous speeches he delivers with Seneca's help.

Nero's marriage to Claudius' daughter Octavia is a mere convenience; he dislikes the sullen, virtuous girl. But then comes the day when Nero falls in love. His choice is a passionate slave girl in the palace, upon whom he showers gifts and a devotion that makes his mother react with fear: What if this girl supplants her? What if she loses her influence to this slave? For once Agrippina loses her head, lashing out and covering her son with scorn for his folly. Then, realizing her mistake, she does an unconvincing about-face and tries to win over the slave girl with presents of jewelry and clothes. In the meantime, Nero falls in love again. Only this time the young woman, Poppaea, will be more than a passing infatuation.

She is not only beautiful but witty, sophisticated, elegant, tasteful, a member of the "fast set" of young Romans from whom Nero has been kept apart by his anxious mother. Poppaea responds to Nero coolly, laughing at the shabbiness of the palace, at his low connection with a slave woman, at Agrippina's political domination. If Nero's first love is uneducated and simple, his second love is a formidable opponent who stings her lover into action with her laughter. Agrippina tries to enlist Octavia as an ally against her son's new mistress, but the girl shrinks from her stepmother, understanding that Agrippina is an enemy.

Agrippina is both skilled and experienced in palace intrigue, knowing a thousand ways to discomfit such a rival as Poppaea. What she has not counted on, though, is the depth of Nero's feeling. Unwilling to permit her to continue slighting his new love, he banishes Agrippina to a country villa not far from Rome. At the same time, as a mark of affection, he chooses the most beautiful and richly jeweled of the robes from the wardrobe of the empresses and sends it to his mother as a gift.

Agrippina is beyond being consoled by mere gifts

when by rights *everything* belongs to her. She rages against her ungrateful son in front of his messengers, sending him hateful letters and threatening to go to the army with Britannicus and appeal to them to right the wrongs she has foolishly committed. She will be destroyed, but she will destroy Nero too, and in that she will find satisfaction. She will make of Britannicus what she made of Nero—emperor!

Nero pretends to ignore the threats, inviting his mother to a banquet, at which he greets her with respect and seats her between Octavia, the wife she had chosen for him, and Britannicus, whose cause she has threatened to champion. Wine is served, heated and spiced, the tasters sipping from all the goblets, as usual. But Britannicus complains, his wine is scalding. Cool water is added, and Britannicus incautiously drinks, not waiting for his taster—a mistake that costs him his life.

Everyone looks on in horror as the youth falls writhing to the floor. "He's having a fit," Nero says blandly, counting on the well-known fact of Britannicus' epilepsy to provide a cover for the murder. He makes a signal to the slaves, and two huge Nubians carry Britannicus away, a pale, pathetic boy. Nothing is said. Nothing has to be said. Agrippina looks searchingly at her son, the echoes of her furious threats can still be heard between them: *I will make of Britannicus what I made of you.*

And this is Nero's answer: He returns Agrippina's gaze steadily and solemnly at this decisive moment in his life. For the murder of Britannicus is not only an act of defiance; it is also one of complicity, of sharing in the blood guilt that is part of his imperial inheritance. It is a gesture of identifying with the mother whom he will kill, whom he must kill to secure his throne. Up until now he has rejected such violence, it being contrary both to his predisposition and to Seneca's teachings. But now he has joined his mother in her dark acts, with a murder that is his rite of passage. The young Nero has come into his own.

Britannicus is buried hurriedly, with the excuse that it is unlucky to prolong the obsequies of a boy who has died before his time. Cosmetics have been applied to cover the characteristic swelling and bruises of the poison, but his funeral takes place in the middle of a sudden storm, which washes off the paint. In any case, there's no disguising his features, which are twisted in a terrible grimace; his death agonies had been severe. All Rome knows what has happened—but all Rome is silent.

After the funeral, Agrippina returns to her country villa to brood on the ingratitude of her son. As a postscript, to make sure there is no mistaking his new power, Nero rapes his mother's young lover Aulus Plautius, whom she had also threatened to raise to the throne, and murders him. Nero sends Plautius' mutilated body to Agrippina with the message "Now let my mother enjoy his kisses." Free of his mother's constraints, the young emperor takes up chariot racing and wrestling in addition to singing and poetry.

For a while Agrippina lives in isolation, deserted by her friends, who want to curry favor with the new emperor. But her craving for power cannot be so easily foresworn, and she secretly keeps in touch with allies she has made among soldiers of the guard. At least that is what is reported to Nero by the prefect Burrhus, an old soldier with a withered hand and a noticeable limp.

Burrhus and Seneca are the two men Nero relies on to help him rule his world-empire, and both are anxious to consolidate their influence. No matter the price, they are determined to prevent Agrippina from making a comeback. Whatever steps she may or may not have taken to regain power, they know it is dangerous to have a woman of her ferocity and cunning as an enemy. Although they were formerly her allies, now she blames them, her son's mentors, for her downfall and openly mocks them as "a cripple and a pedant."

Knowing Nero's habits, Burrhus waits until the young emperor is in his cups before sending Paris, a favorite dancer, to interrupt his revelry with news of Agrippina's "treachery," that she has kept in touch with the guards. Highly emotional in his drunken state, Nero is filled with terror. He summons Burrhus and Seneca for advice, and after much discussion they agree on a plan, a device to get rid of Agrippina secretly: a boat that will collapse at sea.

Agrippina had been lover to her brother and murderer of her husband, but the scheme still goes beyond even her criminal imagination and she never suspects that the invitation Nero sends her is a setup. Instead, flattered by fortune-tellers in Nero's pay, she believes that her return to power is imminent. The feast is a sure sign of it.

It is to be held in Nero's palace on the Bay of Naples, a fashionable resort called Baiae, where hot springs famous for their healing properties draw the cream of the Roman aristocracy. Magnificent estates overlook the water and sprawl on the wooded hills surrounding the bay. Nearby, Agrippina has a villa at Bauli, a smaller resort town also on the water, on an inlet known as the Lucrine Lake. Baiae is a place notorious for luxury and pleasure, for drunken sailing parties and amorous encounters on the beach, which suits Nero's purpose to perfection. He wants to make his mother's death seem accidental, and the disreputable atmosphere lends his scheme an air of probability.

Everything is ready, but just before Agrippina sets out, she is warned by an informer. One of the palace slaves in her pay tells her that Nero is planning to murder her; exactly how, though, has been impossible to discover. Unable to believe the monstrous report and reassured by the gracious style of the invitation, Agrippina decides to ignore the warning as idle gossip. After all, a daily regimen of antidotes, special roots and herbs to counteract even the deadliest toxin, has fortified her system, so if a dish or a drink is poisoned she can afford to take the risk.

The banquet is in the grand Roman style, with Agrippina seated next to her son in the place of honor. A roast pig has been cut open, its stuffing of live quails flying away over the admiring guests. Fish, poultry, and game are served, as well as exotic courses: the tongues of flamingos; sherbets made with snow mixed with light wines; a whole boar stuffed with pheasants, the pheasants stuffed with quails, and the quails stuffed with ortolans. From time to time, guests crowned with roses retire to the vomitorium, where they disgorge what they've eaten so they can continue feasting. Silver lamps burn perfumed oils; the hall is cooled by feather fans moved by slaves; dancers from the East perform to the music of zithers and flutes. And at the end of the dinner, Nero calls Agrippina to come to a place beneath the single rose suspended over the feasting table, a sign of special favor. It is a request for her to remain after all the other guests have departed.*

"Let me kiss your breasts," he whispers to her, "those breasts on which I was suckled." Agrippina smilingly complies, stroking his hair as he fondles her, unconcerned by the waywardness of his act, which she regards only as a measure of the power soon to be hers. It is a theatrical gesture, ironic and unnatural—as indeed all of Nero's behavior

---

*Hence our term sub rosa, literally, "under the rose"—that is, confidential or secret.

becomes from this moment on. It is as if before he can commit the crime he must conceive of it as a work of art; he must interpret it as belonging to the world of Greek tragedy or mythology, where violence is purified by form and incest is associated with the gods.

Plucking the rose hanging overhead, Nero gives it to Agrippina, and watches with tears in his eyes as she leaves the seaside palace. A soldier asks for that night's password. "The best of all mothers!" Nero answers with manic laughter, throwing himself onto the banquet couch, where he waits in a torment of suspense for news of Agrippina's death.

Meanwhile, Agrippina departs in high spirits, rejoicing in her son's renewed affection. She had arrived by land, but a boat has been prepared to take her back across the bay to her villa. Hung with silk, its sides fretted in gold, the ship glides across the calm water like a vision. Agrippina lies on a carved ivory couch next to a friend, Acerronia, a lady-in-waiting, going over the wonderful events of the evening as a freedman massages her.

But suddenly the walls of the cabin begin to sway, and before anyone can move, the ceiling crashes down. The freedman is instantly crushed to death by the heavy lead sheets that have been placed on the roof, but Agrippina and her friend are saved by the high sides of the couch, Agrippina's only injury a badly bruised shoulder. Struggling out from under the debris, she and Acerronia make their way to the deck, which is half submerged in water. The ship is listing dangerously, having been specially prepared to come apart at sea, an idea Nero has taken from an old Roman play. He has again turned to art for inspiration.

All is chaos on the deck, where those sailors unaware of the plot work at cross-purposes with those following Nero's orders to sink the ship. In the midst of the confusion, Agrippina and her lady-in-waiting stumble and fall on the sloping deck, sliding into the water before they are noticed. Agrippina has the presence of mind to cling to the side of the ship, but her friend, thinking to save herself with a lie, tosses frantically in the water shouting, "Help! I am the emperor's mother!"

At the sound of her cries, sailors with long wooden oars rush to that part of the deck nearest the desperate lady-in-waiting, who trustingly reaches out to them. Agrippina, still clinging quietly to the ship, watches as the sailors bring their oars down on her friend's head again and again, beating Acerronia to death. Then the sailors fish the dead woman out of the water and cut off her head as proof, eager to win the rich reward they have been offered for killing the emperor's mother.

It is a chilling moment of realization for Agrippina. Remaining in her hiding place by the side of the ship, she scans the deck: the sailors, the officers, are all foreign. Nero has made sure that not a single ally of his mother's will be among them, that not a single Roman soldier will be present who might try to save her. She is, after all, the daughter of the hero Germanicus, a legendary figure to the army. Looking up at the faces of the Asians, the Nubians, the Egyptians and Greeks, Agrippina sees that her son has anticipated her moves, as only *her* son could.

Still, she is a survivor. Has she lived through the reigns of three emperors, Tiberius, Caligula, and Claudius, only to die during the reign of her son? Summoning her strength, she lets go of the ship, strips off her clothes, and slowly begins to swim toward shore. Although she is a strong swimmer, having had much practice during her exile, her shoulder has been badly hurt and every stroke is painful.

More wounding than the physical pain is the shocking

realization that her son is trying to kill her. She would lift her voice to the gods and call down curses on his unnatural head were it not for the fact that the husband she murdered is now among them (she had had Claudius proclaimed a god and had raised a temple in his honor).

No, Agrippina is alone in the dark water, both physically and spiritually. She herself has broken the bonds of human decency and if she is going to survive she must now draw on whatever reserves of animal strength she has.

Thus it is that a fishing boat comes upon a strange sight in the middle of the Naples Bay: a woman in her early forties swimming by moonlight to the still-distant shore. Calling to her, the crew throws a rope into the water, and Agrippina, exhausted and shivering, climbs out of the water naked. Despite her circumstances she stands with composure on the humble craft, a regal woman, still a beauty, imperious, proud, as she proclaims, "I am the emperor's mother!"

Used to command, Agrippina takes a cloak from the back of a speechless fisherman and orders the boat turned around. And so the former empress arrives at shore bundled in rough garments, sitting amidst baskets of fish and escorted by silent, awed peasants.

Agrippina has been saved, but she knows that her life hangs by a thread. Recovering at her villa, she calculates that for the time being the best course to follow is to pretend ignorance. Revenge can come later. Writing a loving letter to Nero, Agrippina describes the accident and her miraculous escape, sending it with one of her freedmen, whom she instructs to watch her son's reactions carefully.

But Nero knows his mother too well to be fooled, and he finds her expressions of affection more alarming than he would threats. Having Agrippina's freedman seized, he picks up a knife lying next to a fruit bowl and claims that the messenger tried to stab him with it on Agrippina's orders. It does not matter who believes him; what matters is that Agrippina be killed as soon as possible. Once the deed is done, he knows no one will challenge him.

A detachment of guards leaves for the villa, where Agrippina anxiously awaits her son's answer, an answer her slaves have already guessed. One by one they flee, carrying off whatever booty they can. Only a single serving girl remains to keep her mistress company. Thus the soldiers enter the villa without warning and appear in Agrippina's room with drawn swords. Shrieking, the slave is cut down as the soldiers approach her mistress.

"Strike here!" Agrippina cries indignantly, lifting her dress. "Strike the womb that conceived Nero!"

Quickly the soldiers run her through. They wrap her body in a silk tapestry to carry to Nero. The emperor is delirious at the sight. Handling the body limb by limb and commenting on each part as if he were appraising a work of art, he exclaims, "I never knew I had such a beautiful mother!"—a remark that quickly becomes known throughout Rome, repeated by the emperor's aristocratic enemies as a sign of his madness.

The truth is, though, that such behavior is not madness but Nero's way of *fighting off* madness; it is a psychic defense: by turning the corpse into an aesthetic object Nero achieves distance from a crime that would otherwise be unbearable—and that, even so, will haunt him for the rest of his life. On the one hand there is the political necessity of Agrippina's murder, and on the other there is the terrible guilt incurred by matricide, a conflict Nero resolves by "becoming" his mother—on stage. Because, astonishingly enough, the emperor will make his debut in the female role of Agave, a mother who murders and dismembers her son in Euripides' *The Bacchae*.

*   *   *

Nero's procession approaches the enormous Circus. A deafening shout of joy can be heard as the emperor enters, crossing to the imperial box over shimmering sand of *specularia* stone. The structure, six hundred feet long, two hundred feet wide and big enough for 200,000 spectators, is decorated with legendary extravagance: everything is lavish, from the gold nets dividing the audience and the performers, to the amber coffins for those gladiators who die in combat.

The four pontiffs of the sacred colleges appear, resplendent in jeweled robes and carrying images of the gods, which they reverently place upon the *spina,* the wide wall dividing the arena. Their knives glitter in the sun as they slit the throats of the sacrificial animals, the formality of their gestures giving the violent ritual precision and beauty.

In the imperial box, Nero watches with perfunctory attention—he is a skeptic in religious matters, with the exception of a Syrian goddess, Atargatis, whom he venerated for a number of years before losing his faith and publicly urinating on her "divine image." His mistress, Poppaea, is by his side, his wife, Octavia, having long been an object of his scorn.

The imperial "couple" is surrounded by members of the aristocracy in bright jewels and shimmering silks, in white togas bordered with purple, or silver breastplates and waving plumes. Perfume falls on the crowd from censers and scarlet and yellow cloths embroidered with Nero's profile are stretched overhead to protect spectators from the sun.

The chariot races are always first on the agenda and take up at least one day of a festival, which can last twenty, thirty, or even fifty days; Nero's decrees continually extend their length. The horses are well known and beloved among the populace. From stud farms all over the empire, especially Spain, Greece, and North Africa, they are splendid animals, garlanded with flowers, their manes braided with silk and pearls. They are given opulent funerals when their day is done, their epitaphs inscribed in mosaics and engraved on monuments: *Occupavi et vici.*—"I kept the lead and won." *Erupi et vici.*—"I was the outsider and won." *Vincas non vincus, te amamus O Polidoxe.*—"Win or lose, we love you O Polidoxe!"

And their drivers are glamorous figures of the day, so much so as to spur Nero's decision to take part in the chariot races himself in addition to his musical and dramatic performances. Later in his reign, the crowd will go mad with enthusiasm when their emperor drives his chariot to the starting line, the reins in one hand, a whip in the other, his imperial robes exchanged for the short tunic of a common driver, his heels and legs wrapped in linen strips.

It is a dangerous business, too; the axle hub of a competitor can upset a chariot and kill both drivers and all four horses. The turns especially require skill. The chariots must circle the arena seven times, a distance of two and a-half miles, and much depends on the way the two outer steeds are handled, because they are not coupled to the yoke but only attached by a rope. More than one race ends with a driver, a mangled corpse, being dragged out by hooks, or else being carried to a back room to die while his manager curses him and calculates his losses. The winners, though, are crowned with palms, showered with gold—and faced with a new danger, because the women now find them irresistible.

For all his love of Greek art, Nero is still Roman

enough to know that the Circus first and foremost is a place of spectacle. Later he will tour Greece, where he feels the people are more receptive to art and more qualified to judge him. There he will win the prizes at all the festivals, and the Greeks will win freedom from all Roman taxes. His Roman performance, however, will be preceded by death in a thousand forms to delight the crowd, with men pitted against each other and against wild beasts and, on this occasion, against monsters of the deep as well, an artificial lake having been created for the strange creature Nero has introduced to the arena, the octopus. With its huge, infantlike head and its genital-like tentacles, the creature holds a special fascination for the emotionally arrested emperor, who like the octopus is all head and genitals, all intellect and lust.

But the sea monster is just one of many exotic displays. There will be something at the Circus to satisfy every emotion, from awe and wonder to coarse delight. The vestal virgins have been commanded to attend and are placed in the first row to watch the naked gladiators wrestle, a practical joke thought up by the emperor himself. Then there will be the "tortoise," a formation created in the twinkling of an eye by acrobats leaping over their colleagues, their nailed boots sprinkling blood on the shimmering arena's floor. An Egyptian cannibal will consume a fresh human corpse between acts. African elephants will carry turrets filled with gladiators, who will fight each other to the death. And dancers, musicians, and singers will complement the violence.

And so the festival goes, with the populace of Rome assembled day after day in the great Circus, until the races are over and the battles are done and the waters of the artificial lake are red with blood. Only then is the greatest spectacle of all presented to the Roman people. Dressed in a Greek mantle spangled with gold stars over a purple robe, Nero steps out onto the stage and raises his royal voice in sweet, melancholy song, accompanying himself on the lyre.

Thousands listen in hushed awe, and when their emperor finishes his song there is a moment of confused silence, broken at last by thunderous applause. Nero has triumphed! It is the first of many times he will triumph throughout the empire, giving concert after concert for his people. The historians, aristocrats all, record these events with disdain and mockery, emphasizing the ludicrous aspects of his performance—for example, that everyone is afraid to leave the recitals, which go on for hours at a stretch. That guards bar the doors. That officials who fall asleep put their lives in danger. But the "everyone" they talk about means their fellow aristocrats, whose presence at the arena is determined by political necessity. In fact, the concerts make Nero so popular among the rabble that for more than a hundred years his name will be a byword among the commoners, enabling four pretender Neros to raise armies and start rebellions long after he is dead.

But the music is only a prelude to the dramatic recital. Nero's appearance as Agave in *The Bacchae* becomes a kind of roman à clef for the audience, who knows about Agrippina's murder and realizes that the emperor is walking a tightrope between reality and fantasy. If Nero has killed his mother, now the mother avenges herself on the son, his guilt thus purged in an artistic catharsis.

Especially riveting is the last scene, where Agave appears as an ecstatic mother crazed in the drunken service of the god Dionysus. Agave has hunted and killed her son, having mistaken him for a lion, and proudly displays what she thinks is the lion's head to Cadmus, her old father, inviting him to feast on it:

AGAVE   You see? I hold the prize of my hunt, a glory for our family. Take it, Father, and invite your friends to share.

CADMUS: And whose head do you hold in your hands?

AGAVE: A lion's head. Or so the hunters told me.

CADMUS: Look directly at it. Just a quick glance.

AGAVE: What is it? What am I holding in my hands?

CADMUS: Look more closely still. Study it carefully.

AGAVE: No, no! O gods, I see the greatest grief there is.

CADMUS: Does it look like a lion now?

AGAVE   It is—my son's head—I hold—

CADMUS: And mourned by me before you ever knew.

AGAVE: But *who* killed him? Why am *I* holding him?

CADMUS: O savage truth, what a time to come!

AGAVE: For god's sake, speak. My heart is beating with terror.

CADMUS: You killed him.

AGAVE: But where was he killed? Here at home? Where?

CADMUS: He was killed on Cithaeron, there where the hounds tore Actaeon to pieces.

AGAVE: But why? Why had he gone to Cithaeron?

CADMUS: He went to your revels to mock the god.

AGAVE: But we—what were we doing on the mountain?

CADMUS: You were mad. The whole city was possessed.

AGAVE: Now, now I see: Dionysus has destroyed us all.

CADMUS: You outraged him. You denied that he was truly god.

AGAVE: Father, where is my poor boy's body now?

CADMUS: There it is. I gathered the pieces with great difficulty.

(Agave lifts up her son's limbs and mourns each piece separately before placing it on the bier.)

AGAVE: O Father, now you can see how everything has changed. I am in anguish now, tormented, who walked in triumph minutes past, exulting in my kill. And that prize I carried home with such pride was my own curse. How then with these accursed hands may I touch his body? How can I, accursed, hold him to my breast? O gods, what dirge can I sing for every broken limb? . . . Come, Father. We must restore his head to this unhappy boy. As best we can, we shall make him whole again. O, dearest face! Pretty boyish mouth! Now with this veil I shroud your head, gathering with loving care these mangled bloody limbs, this flesh I brought to birth.*

We have, then, the reversal of the young Nero killing his mother and playing the part of a mother who kills her son. But before Nero is through, another inversion will take place. Only this one will occur in "real life," art and life becoming more and more interchangeable for him. The middle-aged Nero, debauched, dissipated in revels that regularly last for twelve hours, will dress in lion skins and attack the genitals of young men and women who are tied naked to pillars.

Thus, through his debauchery and playacting Nero becomes the "lion"-son Agave killed in *The Bacchae.*†

---

*From "The Bacchae" in *Complete Greek Tragedies,* David Grene and Richmond Lattimore, eds. (University of Chicago Press, 1992).

†Nero will become the hero for another artist-debauchee, the Marquis de Sade, a philosopher-playwright who similarly proposed an aesthetic revolution in place of the social one that freed de Sade from the Bastille only to lock him up in a mental institution.

Only now the son is not merely mistaken for a lion but has *become* one—and so survives. Crime and profligacy have degraded him to a bestial level but have also made him strong and invulnerable.

Tyrant of Rome with absolute power over his subjects, Nero is both less than a human being and greater than one, both a beast and a god.

II. STROPHE: A DIVORCE . . . AND A WEDDING GIFT

Nero, secure in his power, wishes to discard his wife, Octavia, the former emperor's daughter. Sullen, brooding over her brother's death, she is virtuous, thoroughly conservative and Roman in her values, a mismatch for Nero although admired among the populace.

The emperor's mistress, Poppaea, is everything that Octavia is not: witty, beautiful, sophisticated, and extravagant. She bathes every day in a mixture of semen and the milk of five hundred donkeys, a beauty treatment her eunuchs are ill-equipped to supply. Empress in all but name, Poppaea incites Nero against Octavia until he is finally ready to act.

Divorcing Octavia on the pretext that she cannot produce an heir—although he does not give her the chance—Nero then trumps up charges of adultery against his faithful wife. But Octavia inspires loyalty in those who know her. Grasping at straws, Nero has her maid put to torture, but the only evidence the inquisitors get is an insult hurled at them from the suffering girl, "My mistress's [obscene; private parts] is cleaner than your mouth!" which stirs up popular sympathy for Octavia in Rome.

There are demonstrations on his wife's behalf, and Poppaea's statue is tumbled from the public places where Nero has honored his mistress. But it is no use. The emperor sends soldiers to Octavia with the order that she commit suicide. Begging for mercy, she is forced to lie down while a doctor opens her veins. And then her severed head is brought to Poppaea as a wedding present.

Twelve days later, she and Nero are married with oriental pageantry and splendor. Nero will marry others before his reign is over, sometimes playing the bride instead of the groom, but he will never marry in greater style. Poppaea is nothing next to him, a supporting actress who knows her place. With his magnificent trappings and his artistic affectations, Nero astonishes the Roman world by both being a Roman emperor and playing one, representing in his godlike person both power and art.

III.   A FIRE, A SONG, AND A MASSACRE

The dog days of summer. The night of July 19, 64. There is a full moon—an important detail, for if Nero had actually planned the great fire that is about to consume his capital he would not have chosen a night when saboteurs could clearly be seen.

The truth is that nobody really knows how it began. At the foot of the Palatine Hill, near the Circus Maximus, shops and storehouses are crowded together, filled with barrels of olive oil and bolts of cloth and all kinds of goods that catch fire easily. A few sparks are all that's necessary to begin the disaster, which by the time it is over will have destroyed two-thirds of the city. The few sparks are fanned into an inferno by a strong wind that spreads the flames, and within moments the wooden seats of the Circus are ablaze with awesome intensity. Chaos ensues, with wild beasts and horses and gladiators, slaves and their masters, acrobats with their trainers, mimes, clowns, dancers, and singers streaming out onto the streets already crowded with citizens and shopkeepers intent on saving their goods.

Soon it is their lives they fight for as the fire encompasses the Esquiline Hill, where the narrow alleys permit the flames to jump from house to house. Everywhere cries of horror can be heard as people are trampled or burned to death trying to rescue loved ones. Men organize to fight the flames, but the streets are filled with collapsing buildings and blinding smoke, making their efforts futile. Many despair and throw themselves into the burning houses where their wives or children have perished. Others are cut off in their attempted flight by a wall of fire that forces them back toward their destruction.

Thieves terrorize those trying to salvage their possessions, and police set fire to mansions in order to loot their treasures. For a full week citizens fight the blaze inch by inch—and just when they seem about to win, the fire suddenly blazes up again with renewed strength.

The Temple of the Moon, dating from the beginning of Rome's history, is destroyed; likewise the Penates, the household gods of Rome, are lost together with the ancient holy trees where the shorn hair of the vestal virgins is displayed. The palace of Numa, the House of Passage, the Nympheum of Claudius, hundred of old books and precious records such as the Sibylline prophecies all go up in flames, which now threaten the sprawling buildings on the Palatine Hill that have become the imperial residence.

Nero rushes from his seaside villa at Antium, thirty miles away. He is in anguish when he hears of the danger to his paintings and statues and objets d'art, to the legendary collections he has gathered by looting the temples of Greece and Asia. Smoke blows across the Palatine from its smoldering southern edges, so that Nero must enter the city from the northeast and make his way through the undamaged Forum. In the face of scorching heat and burning ash, he climbs up to the palace and hurls himself into the rescue effort, forcing his soldiers into the flames to save what they can.

The struggle goes on for days, during which time the emperor makes his headquarters on the other side of the

Tiber. Here he spends hours gazing at his burning capital, until one day, moved by the beauty of the fire and by the sadness of the destruction, he starts to sing, playing a lament on his lyre, an elegy recalling the burning of Troy. It is a sublime moment, but a dangerous one. The masses of refugees, suffering the misery of homelessness and mourning their dead, hear the emperor's song as mockery. Surely Nero himself has ordered the fire; the rumor spreads quickly that the emperor is enjoying the spectacle. And for the first time since the beginning of his reign, the common people are dissatisfied with him. Graffiti are scrawled on the charred walls cursing the emperor. The black sack in which parricides are executed is draped around his image in a public square. A dead child is found exposed in the Velabrum with a message attached: "I do not want to bring you up lest you murder me, my son." And the more Nero sings, the more the people blame him for the fire and whisper that the emperor wants to see the city destroyed.

On the face of it, it is outrageous; yet the rumor gains currency, especially among the refugees, whose misery is greatest. They camp in the temples, the baths, the cemeteries, in the fields around the city, in public squares. Whatever shops or houses are still standing are looted for food. Gangs of slaves without masters roam the streets murdering citizens. Around Nero's headquarters, the guards are given orders to cut down ruthlessly any crowds attempting a coup.

And then, on July 28, just as quickly as the fire has started, it is over. Rubble from demolished houses has been heaped on the Esquiline Hill, creating a huge wall that blocks the fire's path. The blaze is thus forced to feed on itself until it dies.

It is over. And the task of rebuilding the ruined city is daunting. Nero begins by bringing stores of corn from Ostia to feed the homeless at his own expense. The oracles are consulted, the temples are reopened, the statues of the gods are washed with sacred water and wine, and the emperor announces his plans for the "new Rome." Armies of carpenters and workmen are recruited from the provinces, and the work proceeds at an amazing pace, with prizes awarded to the first houses raised amidst the ashes.

Wood is replaced by stone, except for the fixtures; fountains and reservoirs are included in the new public squares; avenues are made broader, houses are set at greater distances from one another. But most important to Nero is a spectacular new palace for himself, to be called the Golden House, which he will build on a vast tract of land taken from the destroyed buildings.

What sets the Golden House apart from other palaces is that here Nero creates a world within a world. This palace is above all a shrine to illusion, to the godlike ability of Art to reproduce the world, to re-create it, to form it according to the human imagination.

This is not immediately apparent, however. On approaching the palace, the visitor first encounters the ostentatious display to be expected in any imperial residence. A colossal statue of Nero, 120 feet high, dominates an imposing courtyard, behind which stretches a seemingly endless row of columns covered in gold.★

★This work of art will have a curious fate. In the reign of Hadrian, thirty elephants will be needed to move the gigantic figure to the Temple of Venus, where Nero will be changed into the sun god Helios, seven rays each thirteen feet long being added to its head. The Circus Maximus, just across the way, will take its nickname, the Colosseum, from the colossal statue, which will continue to stand as late as the seventh century—only with a bearded head of Hercules having been substituted for Nero's ironic, debauched features.

Although that is the largest representation of Nero, the subtlest is a sculpture in Parian marble in the entrance hall that reveals much of Nero's psychology in its face. It is a modern face, frankly interested in the obscene. If there is cruelty in its features, it is not the adolescent sadism of a Caligula but is tempered by something else, a more highly developed consciousness, a tragic sense of life, a sensitivity to beauty. The mouth is shaped not for command but for irony and derision. It is louche, voluptuous. The upper half of the face, with its strong Roman nose and overhanging brow, is the face of a Caesar. The lower half, with its ironically curled lips, its weak chin, its fringed beard, is the face of a satyr. The structure around the eyes, the flat cheekbones, gives the contradictory impression of immaturity and age, of weakness and over-ripeness.

On entering the palace itself, one sees room after room of unparalleled luxury: mosaics of rare marbles and jewels; beds of scented wood, inlaid with mother-of-pearl and covered with silks; baths of sulfur water and seawater brought through special pipes, heated in winter, cooled in summer by snow and ice brought from the mountains; hidden sprays of delicate perfumes from the East; collections of paintings, statues, and rare artwork brought from as far away as China; Nero's golden lyre surrounded by innumerable crowns won in the competitions. The catalog could go on and on; enthusiastic visitors' accounts clearly show that Nero set the standard for extravagance in the ancient world.

In the banqueting hall, fantasy reigns supreme. The sky has been re-created on its huge, domed ceiling, the sun and moon and main constellations depicted in silver and diamonds and gold. Through the clever use of hidden machines turned by running water—a marvel of engineering—

the dome revolves endlessly, revealing the paths of the heavenly bodies as they run their courses and displaying all the attendant shades of light and shadow from "sunrise" to "sunset."

While the heavens revolve above the guests, beneath their feet is a representation of the river Styx with the black frogs of the underworld and the realm of Pluto. And completing the universal scheme, the walls are painted with a vast panorama of the provinces of the empire, its mountains, oceans, and cities.

Stepping from the banquet hall, guests find themselves in another illusion. Nero has created the country in the midst of the city. First come the usual aviaries with exotic birds and the zoos with strange beasts and elegant gardens. But then, the ultimate luxury, stretches a vast expanse of nature: meadows and pastures with sheep and mills, forests stocked with wild animals, ploughed fields and vineyards—all, incredibly, in the midst of crowded Rome.

Wandering in this artfully created nature, a visitor is meant to stumble on all sorts of supernatural illusions. For example, next to a small brook, at the edge of a long field, stands a small rural temple dedicated to Seia, the god of crops. It is made of a hard white transparent stone called *specularia*. When the sun shines on it, it seems as if the light is coming not from a natural source but from within the shrine itself.

The stables are lavish beyond measure, although Nero has not followed the example of Caligula and made his favorite horse a senator, probably because Nero despises the Senate so and does not want to degrade his animals. Remarking on this disdain, Nero's court jester from time to time impudently calls out to the emperor, "I hate you, O Caesar!" And when Nero asks, "Why?" the response, "Because you are a senator!" always gives the emperor a belly laugh.★

Rome becomes a mere suburb at the edge of this vast palatial world-within-a-world. Streets and avenues are rerouted to accommodate the Golden House and its complex of buildings and gardens and fields. All of which seems to give credibility to the rumor that Nero planned the fire to clear the way for his fantastic architectural project.

Still, it is an unlikely charge, if only because so many works of art treasured by Nero have been lost to the flames. Certainly these would have been removed in advance had he ordered the fire. Putting aside the question of guilt, though, it is significant that an emperor should be accused of plotting the destruction of his own capital. The truth is that it is an act of which he is perfectly capable, just as he was capable of killing the woman who gave him life.

To hear Nero rhapsodize about Alexandria only confirms the impression that the vitality of its Hellenic culture makes it the "pearl of the East" for him: its lighthouse is one of the seven wonders of the world; its great library, with thousands and thousands of works, is unique in the civilized world; its philosophical schools are in dynamic ferment; its history is intriguing. The legacy of Greece is more artistic, more enlightened than that of Rome, with

---

★Later, after the treason trials begin, the jester varies this sally by occasionally rebuking the emperor, "You are lazy, O Caesar!" And when the emperor asks, "Why?" he is told "Because you kill the senators one at a time instead of all together!" The remark recalls Caligula's "I wish all Rome had one neck so that I might cut it with a single stroke!"

its inflexible customs and its military spirit. Nero is more Greek than Roman: throughout his reign the great doors of the Temple of Janus, flung open to announce war, remain closed and barred as the emperor pursues his artistic competitions. And so, if the people love him as a *monstre sacré*, they don't forget that he *is* a monster, capable of anything.

Casting about for a solution as rumors and suspicions shake the foundation of his popularity, Nero hits on the strategy of shifting the blame onto the Christians. It is easy to imagine them starting the fire. After all, aren't they hostile to every Roman institution, starting with the gods and ending with the great gladiatorial shows in the Circus? Who more likely to have set the city on fire than these fanatics, with their very un-Roman values and their scandalous religion?

The Christian beliefs turn everything upside down. The last become first, the humble are honored, life is despised and death desired as a passageway to eternity. Whereas the Romans portray children who have died before their time as weeping, having been denied an opportunity for glory, the Christians represent them as joyful angels, having escaped a life of sin and temptation.

In the Roman perspective, on almost every point Christian thinking is perverse and unnatural, with their *god* born in a stable, despised, taunted, crucified. The Roman god Adonis dies, according to pagan mythology, but it is in a boar hunt, not by crucifixion, a death reserved for criminals and thieves, for the lowest of the low. How better to undermine the empire, the social structure, the army, than to allow such a sect freedom?

Thus Nero issues his first edicts forbidding Christians to gather for prayer. Mostly slaves and poor freedmen, with a handful of converts among the nobility, to escape persecution they go underground, inhabiting the catacombs and the grottoes of the Vatican Hill, where they have buried their dead.★ Among them is a man named Paul, a disciple of Jesus who arrived from the East a few years earlier. His denunciation of Rome and Paganism earned him the emperor's enmity. He was brought to Rome in chains by order of Nero, whom he calls "the great enemy," and for two years he has lived under guard near the Forum, weaving ropes and canvas for ships and writing letters to the faithful. Along with Peter, another disciple of Jesus who has taken up residence in Rome, Paul is among the first to be accused of treason by Tigellinus, Nero's pimp and toastmaster and the new commandant of the guards.

Mass arrests begin, with thousands of prisoners crowded into the dungeons of the Circus, where they await the mock trials that will decide their fate. The outcome is a foregone conclusion as senators, pagan priests, philosophers, soldiers, and poets all accuse the Christians. Evidence is given that during the fire ecstatic bands of Christians had chanted hymns of rejoicing and prophesied the end of Rome and the Second Coming of Christ.

The verdict is unanimous: it is the Christians, not Nero, who have destroyed Rome. The judges sentence them to death. Paul, who rejoices at being condemned to the same death as Jesus, is turned head down, with his feet toward the sky to mock him. For days the condemned are tortured in the arena, tied to the backs of angry bulls, tossed to wild beasts, pitted against gladiators. At a feast in

---

★The name "Vatican" antedates the Christian use of it. It derives from *vatis cantus*, Latin for "prophetic songs," since from time immemorial pagan priests and soothsayers delivered oracles under the ancient tree on this hill.

the palace, Nero orders four thousand victims tied to stakes along the garden paths. As the sun sets they are set afire as torches, until the dark paths, the statues and fountains, are illuminated by the blazing bodies. Cries of agony and prayer mingle with drunken toasts as the guests watch the martyrs die.

Outside the palace walls, Christian families kneel in prayer. At dawn they will bargain for the charred remains of their loved ones, offering bribes to the soldiers on guard.

Still in his costume—he has dressed as Apollo for the feast—still drunk on the spectacle of the previous night, Nero plays the lyre and sings, watching indifferently as the bones and ashes are carried away.

Christians will suffer more severely under other emperors, under Diocletian, for example, whose persecutions will be relentless, yet Nero is the emperor identified with the Antichrist of Revelation. He is the Beast of the Apocalypse that "was and is not and yet is," the Dark One, who will be destroyed at the end of time.

It is Nero's love of Greek culture that sets him apart, that turns him into a figure without redemption in Christian eyes. Christianity will ultimately assimilate the sober Roman virtues, even taking over the organizational structure of the Roman empire, its curiae and pontiffs. But the speculations of Greek philosophy, the ecstasies of Greek religion, and the beauties of Greek art will be reserved for the damned, over whom the actor-emperor, Nero, with his golden lyre and theatrical gestures, will always reign supreme.

IV. ANTISTROPHE: BEREAVEMENT . . . AND A VERY SPECIAL "MARRIAGE"

Poppaea is pregnant for the second time. Her first child with Nero, a daughter, died in infancy and was made a goddess, her temple honored by the common people, who bring their humble offerings, and by the politically astute, who lavish great gifts on the shrine.

Now she is again expecting an heir, but the anxiety of carrying the child and the necessary restraints on her pleasures make her quick-tempered.

It is late when the emperor returns from the Circus, where he has watched his favorite horses lose. He is in no mood for her complaints; he has no sympathy for her hardships. Harsh words are exchanged. Poppaea, having long been secure in her husband's admiration, has no fear of him. But that is a mistake, because Nero is lost to any self-restraint. Even the new life in her womb, even the possibility of an heir, does not hold him back. Without thinking, he kicks and beats the beloved wife whose words have angered him. The next moment, he is wild with grief as she dies in his arms.

For weeks he mourns Poppaea, emptying the treasury to bury her in the style of an Eastern queen. But it is not enough. Memories of her will not let him rest. One day he notices a boy named Sporus, who looks remarkably like her, feature for feature. From a certain angle, in a certain light, it would not be possible to distinguish Sporus from Nero's dead wife.

So a certain operation is performed: the boy is castrated and his name changed to Sabina, after Poppaea's family name. He is dressed in Poppaea's jewels and robes and veils and publicly married to Nero in a feast that lasts for days, with gold and food distributed to the poor and Nero singing his own love poems to the guests.

The Senate, the foreign ambassadors, the chief officers of state, all congratulate their emperor on his good fortune. "Nothing is impossible for Nero!" his enemies assure him—behind his back wishing his father had made such a marriage. It is a joke that will cost them their lives.

V.   TO DIE LIKE A ROMAN

**No matter how many men you kill, you can never
kill your successor.**
           —Seneca's remark to his pupil Nero

Nero's life from here on is a postscript, tiresome, pre-
dictable, the end inevitably following from the beginning.
Nero becomes a parody of himself, a ruler whose choices
are limited by his obsessions and whose natural exuber-
ance is obscured by his fears.

He will enter into marriage with a woman, a wealthy
widow, but this marriage will have little meaning. It is the
boy Sporus who will be with him to the end.

The concerts continue, in both Italy and Greece,
where, pathetically, Nero buys off rivals whose voices are
better than his. On one occasion he even has his guards
kill a singer who haggles too long before withdrawing.
Desperate to win, and in denial that his victory is assured
because he is emperor, Nero works himself up into a state
of nerves before each performance, depending on his stage
manager to soothe and reassure him before he can perform.

As an actor, he adds roles to his repertoire. A favorite is that of a pregnant woman giving birth. And if his ever-watchful guards disapprove of their emperor's shrieking and frantic tossing about with birth pangs, they nevertheless form a claque to ensure the applause Nero craves.

His continued devotion to his art and to sexual debauchery, and his continued indifference to military glory, mean that during his entire reign Rome is at peace: Nero has neither the interest nor the time for war. Not that the peace is maintained by mere passivity. No, Nero insists that Rome's authority remain undiminished throughout the world, and he shows great skill in diplomatic maneuvering.

When there is trouble with Parthia over Armenia, for example, he resolves the issue first by threatening force and then by dazzling his opponent with spectacle. He has Corbulo, his best general in Asia, rigorously prepare the "soft," peacetime army stationed in the East. They are taken from their comfortable quarters in Syria, with its mild climate, and sent to the inhospitable Armenian mountains. Here they spend the winter in high-altitude camps training in light clothes and with scant provisions. By the time spring arrives, the weak have been killed by frostbite and privation while the rest have been hardened into a formidable fighting force. Ready for battle, they are positioned for attack on the Parthian border under the admirable generalship of Corbulo.

But Nero does not order attack. Instead he issues an invitation to Tiridates, the Parthian candidate for the Armenian throne, offering him safe conduct to Rome. If Tiridates will submit to the yoke of the Roman emperor, Nero suggests, then he will be permitted to rule Armenia despite his ties with the king of Parthia, his brother.

It is a clever bargain. Tiridates is brought to Rome at Nero's expense, and at every stage of the journey he and his followers are overwhelmed by examples of Roman might and wealth. The climax occurs in the capital, where Nero outdoes his own legendary extravagance in a display that dazzles the Parthian visitor with its grandeur. And the impression made is so lasting that for the next fifty years there will be peace with Parthia, an enormous advantage to Rome both economically and militarily.

Not only in foreign affairs does Nero rise to the responsibility of ruling the empire. Some of his domestic projects and decrees reveal wisdom and even humanity. Hearing that masters have taken to abandoning their sick and aged slaves, for example, he puts the wealthy under a legal obligation to pay for the care of their slaves and gives slaves the right to lodge complaints against their masters.

Set against such generous impulses, though, is Nero's fear for his life, making him forget his humanity and driving him further and further into the role of tyrant. In the beginning of his reign, the measures the young emperor takes to safeguard his throne are severe yet in touch with reality. But after he uncovers the Pisan conspiracy in the year 65, his decrees become extreme and unjust.

Not that the conspiracy is dangerous or effective. It is led by Piso, a young nobleman passively attracted to power but without the will to make a serious effort to achieve it. A huge soldier in the guard is to throw himself at Nero's feet and wrap his arms around his knees in supplication when the emperor comes to the Circus. While Nero is being held thus, Piso's confederates are to stab him in the back. Serious or not, the plot triggers Nero's insecurity, and the list of traitors grows in proportion to the emperor's terror, those whose guilt is probable joining those whose guilt is proved.

Nero's old teacher and adviser Seneca, retired from public life, will perish in the aftermath of the scandal, because he has frequently been observed visiting the conspirators. Postponing his death with endless moral platitudes, the old philosopher will finally have to be silenced by the soldier sent with the order that he commit suicide by slitting his wrists.

Since Seneca is as close as Nero comes to having a father figure, Nero's remarks on his death are especially revealing. When the soldier returns to the palace with the news of the suicide, Nero tells his courtiers, "He was envious and grasping. He loved riches. He was lustful. He heaped up wealth by any means. He imposed unfair taxes and stole from innocent victims. He betrayed friendships. He was fawning in exile and proud and selfish in power. He was devoted to only one person, himself. Yes, he was all this. And he was my mentor."

The speech is problematic and cuts two ways. Despite the seeming harshness of the negative eulogy, Nero ends by identifying himself with Seneca—"He was my mentor." By doing so, he is calling himself a student of falsehood, a liar, thus negating the catalog of Seneca's faults. If Nero is Seneca's student, we cannot believe him when he criticizes Seneca. It is a version of the ancient paradox "All Cretans are liars—and I am a Cretan," in which the speaker invalidates his own proposition.

Nero's speech is like a cipher, which can be read in many different ways. But if we decode his hidden message, we discover that he is paying an inverted compliment to Seneca, the mentor-father who helped him through the first years of his reign. It is as close as the emotionally arrested aesthete can come to expressing feeling directly.

The Pisan conspiracy is only the first of several plots to kill Nero, all of which are halfhearted and come to nothing; they are revealed by the emperor's spies or by untrustworthy slaves or faithless friends or gossiping courtesans. The main damage they do is to make Nero see danger everywhere, so that soon the innocent join the guilty among the accused. Just as the tallest tree draws lightning, an illustrious family background or great wealth or popularity is enough to condemn a man or a woman to death as the potential rallying point for a coup. Even the young children of such "traitors" must be killed. They are future enemies, the girls as well as the boys. Only, there is this difference: the girls must be deflowered first, since it is against Roman tradition to execute a virgin. Even Poppaea's child from her first marriage is killed, a little boy whose crime it is to have played at being emperor.

An indictment can be drawn up on the most frivolous grounds: "When the emperor suffered from a bad cold which endangered his glorious voice, the noble senator Thrasea did not take part in the sacrificial offerings for his recovery."

Slights, insults formerly overlooked, are now remembered: A senator known for the probity and virtue of his life had refused to join his colleagues in congratulating Nero on the death of his mother. The man is condemned to death.

Some die nobly, taking courage from the long Roman tradition of honorable suicide. The young poet Lucan, first brought into disfavor because he mocks Nero's poetry, opens his veins in a hot bath and then suddenly thinks of a description of death he would like to include in his unfinished poem *Pharsalia*. Beckoning to a friend, he dictates seven additional lines, instructing that they be added to his work.*

The writer Petronius, a companion in the emperor's debauches, reveals too many secrets of Nero's orgies in his ironic epic, *Satyricon* (where it is possible to see Nero as the gross and foolish Trimalchio). Commanded to die, Petronius first prepares copies of his work and sends them to a friend for safekeeping. Then he invites a fellow writer and a philosopher to a banquet, at which they discuss the nature of life while he opens his veins and bleeds. He then bandages his wrists to continue his discussion awhile, savoring death as he would a fine wine. As a final gesture, just before the witty author loses consciousness he smashes a priceless cup the emperor has been coveting, and smiles as he dies—perhaps because he has deprived Nero of the treasure; perhaps at the thought of the letter he has written his imperial "friend," a document filled with insults and mockery.

In this Petronius is unusual, for most of those condemned heap praise on the emperor in their wills, hoping that, flattered, he will allow their families to inherit their estates. Wherever Nero goes, he is met by the victims' relatives kneeling in the street, on the steps of the senate, near the temples. They throw themselves at his knees and try to kiss his hands, afraid that they themselves might soon join the ever-growing numbers of exiles languishing on small islands in the Aegean Sea.

Putting aside the exiles, just the list of the condemned in one month is impressive. Take the month of April—renamed Neroneus, a tag that never caught on. The tribune

---

*Lucan, *Pharsalia*, Canto III, 641.

of a praetorian cohort, along with a centurion, two old-fashioned soldiers, curse "the actor Nero" and are killed for it. The tribune dies like a soldier, coldly appraising the sword about to sever his head. Then there are two senators, Flavius and Scevinus—motives for treason obscure. And Afranius Quintanus, whose bad character leads him to rebellion. And Senecio, a childhood friend, likewise of no account. And Volusius of the Imperial Navy commits treason against the emperor by saying he has been insufficiently rewarded for his part in Agrippina's death—and on and on. The list is endless.

For a short while there is a pause. Nearly forty thousand die in a plague that touches nearly every family in the city. The smoke of funeral pyres blackens the skies. But when the epidemic is over, the executions begin again and continue until the day Nero loses his throne.

FEBRUARY 68. Nero returns triumphantly from his tour of Greece, crowned with a wreath of wild olive leaves and carrying the Pythian laurel. A revolt among the troops in Gaul, when he first hears of it, troubles him less than some difficulty he has been having with his voice. Later it will be noticed that the rebellion has broken out on the anniversary of Agrippina's death, but at the time, Nero thinks only of his Greek triumph, of the 1,800 laurel crowns he has won in the poetry and music competitions.

Vindex, a native of Gaul whose father had been made a senator by Claudius, is behind the unrest. Having been raised in Rome but conscious of his foreign background, Vindex is "more Roman than the Romans" and cannot tolerate Nero's betrayal of the imperial ideal. Returning to Gaul, Vindex works tirelessly to make the officers ashamed of serving under "a singer and a madman." Furthermore,

Nero's execution of the admired general Corbulo after his faithful service in Armenia and Syria proves that no one is safe from the emperor's suspicions. Under Nero, loyalty is rewarded by death, Vindex warns his fellow soldiers, while honor is given to harp players, eunuchs, and whores.

Urgent letters describing the growing danger are sent to Nero, who is attending athletic games in Naples. For eight days the letters are left unopened, eight days during which Vindex has time to gather support. Having won over the troops in Gaul to the rebellion, Vindex now sends messages to Galba, the governor of Spain, trying to woo him by offering him the throne.

Advanced in years, Galba is a man of simple tastes, with a long career of distinguished service behind him. Vindex knows that Galba's patrician connections and his reputation for effective rule in Africa as well as Spain will attract many followers, for the old man represents Roman tradition and a vindication of the Senate.

Galba is undecided, but events force his hand. Vindex's messages to him are intercepted by Nero's spies, and the emperor immediately orders that Galba be put to death for treason. Galba throws in his lot with Vindex, and when an army sent from Rome decides not to oppose the rebels but to join them, Nero's fate is sealed.*

Thus the world learns a new lesson: that a Roman emperor can be chosen not only in Rome but also in the provinces. It is a dangerous lesson for the future of the empire. It emphasizes the importance of the individual gen-

---

*In the single year following Nero's death, three emperors will have short, unstable reigns: Galba, Otho (Poppaea's first husband, sent to the provinces with the army when she became Nero's mistress), and Vitellius.

erals, it implies a decentralization of power, and after
Nero's death it will lead to civil wars as destructive as the
ones that raged during the Republic.

But even at this critical juncture, Nero is not alive to
the danger threatening him. He agrees to return to Rome
from Naples, but he makes the trip in a leisurely manner,
stopping off on the way to inspect a newly invented musical instrument that intrigues him, a hydraulic organ.
When he finally does arrive at the palace he ignores the
warnings of a delegation from the Senate, switching the
topic instead to the new organ, which he will install in
the Circus, "if Vindex will allow" him, he jokes.

Galba, supported by the armies of Spain and Gaul,
marches toward Italy as Nero performs in *Oedipus in
Colonus*. It is taken as a bad omen that he slips and falls on
the stage while declaiming, "Wife, mother, father, all force
me to my end. . . ." And indeed it is to be his last public
performance.

His final days are spent making all kinds of feverish
plans, which he takes up at one moment only to discard at
the next. Their impracticality is a measure of his desperation. He will go to Gaul himself, he vows, and appeal to
the rebels with a speech that will move them to tears.
"That is the advantage being an actor," he says. The next
moment, it is to Parthia he will travel. Surely, the Parthian
king will give him refuge in consideration of the peace he
has concluded with him. Or perhaps he should wait for
Galba to enter Rome and then embrace him as a brother?
Nero would be quite content to abdicate if given the gov-
ernorship of Egypt, he tells his boy-wife Sporus, who
faithfully clings to him. "Leave the Romans to the rule of
Galba," Nero complains bitterly, "for they deserve each
other."

As the rebels approach the capital, the Golden House

is deserted by all but a handful of slaves. Wandering through the empty, magnificent rooms, Nero pauses, lost in a reverie, before his 1,800 victor's crowns from the Greek competitions. Phaon, a loyal freedman, suddenly appears with more disastrous news to shock him back into reality. The praetorian guard, falsely informed that Nero has fled, have switched their allegiance to Galba. There is no time to lose—Nero must leave the city immediately.

Together with Sporus, a few slaves, and the freedman Phaon, the emperor manages to make his way to the Colline Gate to the north of the city, hiding his well-known features behind a cloth. Mounting horses, they ride out into the open country, through a marshy, brush-covered land, until they reach Phaon's small house amidst the reeds. Here Nero waits in the garden, dipping his hand in a puddle of muddy water and drinking from his palm, as Phaon breaks open a ventilation hole at the back of the house so the emperor can crawl through.

Epaphroditus, one of the loyal slaves who have gone into hiding with their master, pleads with Nero to commit suicide, telling him that the Senate has proclaimed the deposed emperor a public enemy and decreed that he shall die "in the ancient Roman method of execution." When Nero asks what that is, Epaphroditus answers that it is to be stripped naked and whipped to death. Hearing this, Nero picks up a dagger to try its point against his chest. But he cannot bring himself to plunge it in, so he crawls into the house together with his slaves and his boy-wife.

Sporus chants a prayer. Phaon finds a mat for Nero to rest on and brings him some food, but Nero cannot eat. Instead he asks the slaves to dig a grave for him there in the mud floor of the room. As they work, the sound of galloping horses can suddenly be heard nearby. Realizing that soldiers have come in search of him, Nero grabs up the dagger and plunges it into his throat. *"Qualis artifex pereo!"* he murmurs as he lies dying—*"What an artist is lost in me!"*

IVAN THE TERRIBLE

I. THE WIDOW'S INHERITANCE

I am a mad, stinking dog.
—Ivan the Terrible

THE YEAR 1566. A sinister monastery in the midst of dark woods far to the north of Moscow. In rows of bare stone cells, the "monks" are getting up for prayer and pulling on their coarse brown robes. Only they are not monks at all. A roll call would reveal them to be the most infamous murderers and torturers in sixteenth-century Russia. They are the *oprichniki,* "those set apart," men Ivan has chosen from among the powerless and raised to a position above the law on the condition that they take part in his savage crimes.

The *oprichniki* walk solemnly down the long, silent corridors to services, their faces both cunning and cruel. They need to be crafty to survive in the world of Ivan's court, where one false step will land them in the position of their victims. There is no telling what the tsar will require of them or how he will react at any given moment. A joke might be told at dinner. Ivan is delighted and doubles over with laughter. Suddenly, still laughing, he reaches for a knife and cuts off the jokester's ear, intently peering into his eyes for a sign of rebellion or pain. But no, the man is Ivan's, he belongs to the Tsar body and soul and can only thank his master for punishing him as he deserves. Because of his absolute obedience, the man survives, saving the life of his family and friends; because when Ivan kills those he deems unfit, he destroys root and branch— parents, children, brothers, servants, companions—leaving no one to take revenge.

With such control, Ivan has fashioned his band of *oprichniki* into a political tool he uses brilliantly. Assured of his followers' loyalty, he can let them loose on the country like savage dogs. In fact, the dog's head and the broom are their emblems: the dog to destroy, the broom to sweep away the enemies of the Tsar. If they murder the innocent as well as the guilty, so much the better. The more cruel and more arbitrary they are, the more Ivan is delighted. Like Stalin four hundred years later (a great admirer of Ivan's), he understands that for terror to be effective no one must feel safe: *Today* he *is the one strung up to die; tomorrow it might be* me.

But although Ivan does calculate the effects of the terror he has unleashed, it would be a mistake to see him as coldly calculating. For despite the Tsar's brilliance, despite his mastery of diplomacy, his military triumphs, and the great reforms he masterminds, he is mad. There is no question about that. The acts of torture he inflicts daily would be classified today as criminally insane. Husbands are flayed alive or slowly roasted to death while their wives and daughters are brutally raped before their eyes; princes are impaled on stakes while needles are driven under their fingernails; sons are ordered to kill their fathers and then are themselves executed as parricides; bishops are thrown to hungry bears; children are ripped from the wombs of pregnant women; and young girls are stripped naked to be used for target practice.

So we have the spectacle of a criminal madman ruling Russia for more than forty years, and his reign is not a mere aberrancy but a central one. Ivan will set his country on the course it will follow through Soviet times: the secret informers; the torture chambers; the treason trials; the mass executions of his own people—sixty thousand inhabitants of Novgorod are put to death in one week—the lust for world domination.

All the tactics of repression the Soviets will still employ in Russia four hundred years later are put in place under this Tsar—who at the same time is an intellectual and a subtle theologian. He successfully debates both the pope's emissaries and Lutheran ambassadors, advocating Russian Orthodox Christianity with great eloquence. His logic and learned arguments would make it simple to believe in his sanity were it not for the fact that always at hand is his iron-tipped staff. His knuckles grow white as he grasps it, and there is always the possibility that at any moment he will lunge forward and strike his opponent dead, as he will, among others, his own beloved son in a fit of rage.

We must, then, take Ivan's madness as our starting point, at the same time not discounting the possibility that there is a method to it. For with his reign of terror, he has managed to destroy the ancient aristocracy whose internal squabbles have weakened the nation. Powerful nobles, Church leaders, wealthy magnates are all humbled into dust. With a single decree, Ivan has dispossessed the princes and given their lands to his chosen henchmen, the *oprichniki*. Twelve thousand of Russia's leading families trudge through the snow in the dead of winter to faraway villages. Their vast estates surrounding Moscow become part of a private kingdom within a kingdom, the land of the *oprichniki*, the Tsar's own creatures.

All the bloodshed and torture have given him unquestioned authority as a ruler. With every voice of opposition silenced, Ivan can concentrate on turning Russia into a great empire, a major player on the world stage. And yet it is a delicate balancing act: we must not forget that Ivan has become addicted to the spectacle of murder.

Ivan himself understands that his soul is diseased, and in a fit of remorse—or could it be boasting?—calls himself "a mad, stinking dog," a sinner who begs the holy fathers of the Church to chastise him. But woe to the rash man who takes him at his word! Because he cannot help himself: inflicting suffering has become as necessary to him as air or food, or prayer, which for Ivan is a passion as all-consuming as his vices.

Which brings us back to that dark monastery in the midst of the woods, where his henchmen have gathered for the arduous services that last from four until eight in the morning. One by one, Ivan's lieutenants assume their favored places in the chapel, the most prominent among them his favorite, Malyuta ("Stumpy") Skuratov, whose presence is somewhat ironic considering he has strangled the head of the Russian Church with his bare hands. All await Ivan, who rises slowly from a troubled sleep, more exhausted than the night before. Three blind old men have taken turns watching by his bed. They whisper legends and poems to soothe him as he tosses and turns fitfully.

Since the death of Anastasia, the wife of his youth, he has been in torment. For thirteen years she had brought peace to his soul. Kind to the poor, merciful to the condemned, she inspired him to "live in the light." Her death does not make Ivan lose his faith in God, but his conception of God changes: God is indifferent to human misery, and his justice is beyond all human conception. *Search for God and His strength, seek His Face continuously;* the words of the Psalmist sink deep into his consciousness; and Ivan does search, finally discovering a God who is beyond good and evil.

This will remain true of him during every crisis in his long reign: in all adversity, he sees the hand of God, which is perhaps what gives him his strength. When the Crimean khan burns Moscow to the ground, when Ivan's capital is in ruins and thousands lie dead, with the rivers polluted by charred corpses, he calmly answers his adversary's taunts and insults: "The khan has done nothing! It is God who punishes me for my sins." He mobilizes all his energies and speedily oversees the rebuilding of the city. His wife's death may turn him to debauchery and cruelty—he gives himself up to the long-suppressed penchant for cruelty that is so strong in him—but his faith never wavers. He takes his heavy burden of misery and sin to his Creator, arising in the middle of the night to stand for hours before the mystic icons in a trancelike state of prayer and contemplation.

The liturgy begins in the chapel and a hush falls over the "brethren" as their royal "abbot" strides through the crowd. He looks to neither the left nor the right but prostrates himself on the stone floor. Groaning, and begging for forgiveness, he smashes his head against the paving stones again and again. His calloused and bruised forehead becomes a common sight at the Russian court; foreign ambassadors are told to take no notice of it.

But it is impossible to conceal that something extraordinary is going on in Russia. Seeing the steady flow of refugees streaming over the border, the king of Poland, Sigismund Augustus, asks the Russian envoy, "What is the *oprichnina?*" and is told that no such brotherhood exists.

Far from believing this, Sigismund imagines that Russia is ready to revolt. Hearing that the Tsar spends half his time in prayer, he decides that it is a good time to strike.

He is greatly mistaken, however. Ivan's troops win victory after victory in Livonia, a disputed land near the Baltic, forcing the Polish king to sue for peace. When Ivan turns from his prayers to affairs of state, he is razor sharp. Furthermore, Sigismund has misunderstood the effect of the Tsar's withdrawal to his "monastery." He imagines that Ivan is out of touch with events, but in reality the Tsar's retreat has strengthened his position in Russia. Strangely enough, there is no better way to prepare the nation for the *oprichnina* and its reign of terror than the one Ivan has chosen: a mysterious retreat. Without any warning, he packs up the state treasury, the heavy gold plates and jeweled goblets and precious icons, and together with his chosen favorites leaves Moscow, heading out to the north on sleds.

Word races through the city: the Tsar is deserting them. "Where is he going?" the question is anxiously asked. "Wherever God leads," is the only reply he gives. Only after days of travel does Ivan fix on a hunting lodge in the trackless wilderness, which feverish construction turns into a monastery and fortress. From this retreat, he informs the nation that he is sick of the treachery on every side and that he is leaving them for good.

The common people are in an uproar. They are ready to riot and tear the aristocrats to pieces. Under the benevolent influence of his wife, Ivan had instituted reforms to relieve the burdens of the poor, the peasants, and the merchants. They have no inkling how Ivan will change as a result of Anastasia's death: that when he returns two months later, his hair and beard will have been pulled out, that he will be stooped and trembling, his features contorted in a nervous tic, his eyes vacant and staring. At this time, he will start to be known as *grozny*—terrible, fearsome, awful in his might. But all the people know now is that their father has left them. How can Russia exist without its tsar?

Government officials, nobles, and Church fathers hurriedly form a delegation. They take the trip over marshy bogs and through dense forests to plead with Ivan, who professes no desire to return. "Moscow is a viper's nest," he tells them. "I am surrounded by treachery and lies." A possibility, but only a possibility, is finally held out. He might reconsider if he could be sure all traitors will be punished. But there must be a new understanding: none of his plans must be opposed. The mildest criticism must be suppressed. Even the Church, which traditionally intercedes for mercy, must in the future remain silent.

One delegation after another comes from Moscow to beg him to resume power. But he is no hurry; he dallies. He indulges in the fantasy of abdication, and at the same time, he tests his power; he flaunts it, he increases it by forcing the people to woo him. Will he or will he not return to save Russia?

This is another instance where pathology and policy are almost indistinguishable. The mock monastery Ivan creates is a version of a recurring obsession, to give up the throne and become a monk (as he will finally do on his deathbed, when he is given the name Brother Jonah). This impulse is manifest throughout his life: time and again he will make pilgrimages to faraway monasteries, seeking the advice of "holy fools" and saints, which he prizes above that of his closest advisers. He has even had a cell prepared for him in a hermitage on the edge of the arctic circle. He hopes that one day this cell will be his "palace." So the retreat from Moscow is both a clever strategy and a form of religious mania. As a political ploy, it puts the nation in the palm of his hand. Yet the tsar genuinely longs to abdicate.

In fact, on two other occasions Ivan will publicly give up his crown. The first time, he dresses the old and venerable Prince Fedorov in royal robes and sets him on the throne: "Here! You have what you desire!" he declares, bowing low before Fedorov as if with deep respect for the old man's lifetime spent in service. "But what I have given, I can take away," he adds, stabbing him to death the next moment. Thus Ivan, who lives in constant fear of assassination, assassinates the mock-tsar he has created. And then, purged of dread, he resumes the throne.

The second time Ivan abdicates, however, the drama lasts longer. For an entire year, he sets a young, recently baptized Tatar prince in his place, whose duty it will be to perform all the royal ceremonies. While reserving to himself the significant decisions, Ivan moves from the palace to a small house and humbly petitions the new "Tsar" for his needs. He praises the young man and gives way before him in public, until finally, tiring of the farce and unable to bring himself to renounce power, he resumes the crown, sending his substitute off to obscurity after his year of glory.

In that choice of a Tatar substitute lies a world of significance, revealing as it does Ivan's unconscious identification with Russia's enemies. At its birth, Russia was crushed beneath the heel of cruel Asiatic invaders; for over two centuries, from the 1200s until the 1400s, the Mongols, the Tatars, held Russia back in the dark ages while western Europe advanced in culture. And although Ivan finally puts an end to the threat, taking the Tatar strongholds Kazan and Astrakhan and assimilating their people, he also assimilates their savagery.

The double-headed eagle, the symbol of Russian tsardom, looks both to the East and to the West, to Asia and to Europe, to the past and to the future. And this eagle is a symbol of Ivan as well. Because although he tries to create a modern state, although he is fascinated by Western thought and European technology, the atavistic, the destructive cling to his soul. Just as the nomadic Asian hordes brought nothing but desolation to whatever crossed their path, by the end of Ivan's reign the countryside around Moscow will be desolate, its population butchered or fled far from their most *Christian?* their most *savage?* Tsar.

We have only to return to the monastery where we have left Ivan deep in prayer to be confronted with this duality in its starkest form. His morning devotions over, the tsar spends the afternoon on state affairs. There is a sense of relief, a respite from the high emotions of religious fervor. Perhaps foreign visitors have arrived. The English are just discovering Russia during this time, and Ivan, instantly an Anglophile, pursues the possibility of marriage to Queen Elizabeth—who is not above humoring him with coy, charming letters in the interest of British trade. Perhaps another Muscovite delegation has shown up begging him to forgive his unworthy subjects and return to the capital. Or it might be that Siberian explorers seek an audience, eager to lay their gifts of furs and gold at his feet.

But as the afternoon wanes, Ivan grows restless with these mundane occupations and finally breaks away. He descends to the torture chambers, where his savage instincts can be satisfied just as his sublime impulses found their outlet in prayer. Splattered with blood, his face flushed with ecstasy, the Tsar staggers from victim to victim crying *"Hoyda! Hoyda!"* to the torturers, an expression the Tatars use to urge on their horses, fitting words for a man bent on ruling Russia with the ferocity of a beast of prey. Yet the irony is that beneath this throwback to Tatar brutality lies the personal suffering of an inconsolable husband. "Your only resemblance to a human being is your physical shape," writes Prince Kurbsky, a defector who has fled to Poland and who, from the safety of exile, accuses Ivan of a long list of crimes. (Their correspondence will continue for eight years, a kind of propaganda war, won by Kurbsky, although his letters do not match Ivan's brilliant rhetoric or learning. The word was out about the Tsar, and Europe devoured the accounts of Ivan's atrocities.)

For the most part, Ivan's letters to Kurbsky are eloquent and forceful summaries of sixteenth-century political theory; in his exposition of the duty owed the state, he draws extensively on the Bible, history, and Classical philosophy. However, there is a significant cri de coeur in one passage where Ivan lets down his guard. Kurbsky has charged him with the death of many loyal men (as Stalin will in the 1930s, Ivan has executed his best generals).

As Ivan tries to justify his actions, or at least to prove that Prince Kurbsky is no judge of them, his first wife, Anastasia, suddenly comes to mind. In a pathetic non sequitur, Ivan seems to be thinking out loud when he speaks of her: "Why did you take my little heifer from me?" he writes, using the popular term of endearment *yunitsa* when referring to Anastasia. "If only you had left her alive!" he laments, although the one person who may have "taken" Anastasia was Ivan himself. He had forced her to go on an arduous pilgrimage in the dead of winter to a monastery far to the north. The monks, rigorous ascetics, were unable to provide the simplest comforts when she fell sick. Anastasia would return to Moscow alive, but she would never recover. "If only you had left her to me, then none of this would have happened . . . ," Ivan concludes emotionally, revealing much in this personal aside.

His words are moving, but how can we explain their logic? If Kurbsky and his fellow traitors have "taken" Anastasia from him, it could only have been by poison. That is the implication. Ivan could not have believed that, however, since no one was punished for her death, and we can be sure that if he had suspected poison at the time, there would have been a bloodbath. Furthermore, Kurbsky only fell out of favor sometime later—because of a military defeat, for which Ivan blamed him—so there is no chance Ivan could have connected him with Anastasia's death.

But emotions have a deep life of their own, little concerned with objective facts; their logic is a subjective one, their narratives, their chronologies, those of a dream. In his suffering, Ivan conflates the figures of his mother and his wife. When he was a boy of eight, his mother was poisoned by scheming nobles who envied her power. And now, twenty-two years later, we see Ivan imagining that these same enemies, long since dead, have also destroyed his beloved Anastasia.

The same fantastic leap over time and place is to be seen in the creation of the *oprichniki*. It is true enough, as we have noted, that they spread terror far and wide, consolidating the tsar's power. But at the same time that they perform this political task, they perform the "dream task" of avenging Anastasia's murder. Ironically, the name that Ivan has given them, *oprichnina,* not only means "those set apart" but has a secondary, more obscure meaning: "the widow's inheritance." And most certainly this demonic band is an "inheritance." They are the "inheritance" of his grief, while Ivan himself, bereft and bloodthirsty, is the "widow." "Why have you taken my little heifer from me?" we can hear him roar in the monastery as his henchmen roam out across the land, their violence and cruelty an expression of his sorrow.

II.   THE GAMBLE

Did He Who made the lamb make thee?
—William Blake

THE YEAR 1538. A young boy is left to shift for himself in the gloomy palace of the Kremlin. His father has been dead since he was three. When he is eight his mother is poisoned, and her lover, who may have been his real father, is put to death. Even the child's beloved nurse is taken from him; his cries and pleas echo in the great halls of the fortress as she is brutally dragged away, for the nobles leave no one alive who is loyal to the boy.

Sometimes he is hungry and cold, because no one bothers about his meals or cares whether he has enough warm clothes for the severe Russian winter. His only companion is his deaf-mute brother. In fact, his life would be more secure if he were a deaf-mute himself, for what he sees in the Kremlin will not bear repeating.

Such is Ivan's childhood.

The great nobles, divided into two factions, fight their way to power only to be displaced in a continuous game of musical chairs: first the Shuiskys, then the Belskys, then the Shuiskys again, on and on. There will be time to kill the child once one or the other party is securely in power. But neither side achieves a final victory and it is perhaps for this reason that Ivan survives.

So he lives, neglected and lonely, his life hanging by a thread. On ceremonial occasions he is dressed in cloth of gold and set on a throne in the cathedral, but in private, the state robes are stripped from him and he is treated with contempt by the conniving, murderous nobility. He learns that power has two aspects, blood and splendor, and that each is intoxicating, each sublime.

Ivan's character is formed by this contradiction: while at one moment the young prince is hailed as the hope of Russia, covered with jewels and paraded before the people, at the next he is just an orphan boy, a nuisance whose meager dinner will be forgotten when the servants are busy and whose very life depends upon his insignificance. He is everything, yet he is nothing.

This double sense of who he is will find expression in Ivan's humility before God—he is *"but a passing shadow upon the face of the earth"*—and his arrogance before humanity, upon whom he tramples, "as befits *the heir of Caesar."* Even before Ivan receives any formal tutoring, he is drawn to the beauty of the liturgy, the otherworldly chant that proclaims human frailty and yet lauds the majesty of God's anointed, the tsar.

These ideas become real for the young Ivan; they are mysteries grasped amidst the icons and the martyrs' relics in the dark Kremlin churches. And although he will have regular lessons in the Bible and history and even Classical logic, though a prolonged period of study follows, these strong first impressions remain formative. Throughout his life, Ivan never untangles thought and passion. For him, abstract ideas and bookish logic will never have the significance of the senses and the emotions. His early experiences form his outlook, while books merely provide the evidence for what he already knows.

Perhaps fortunately, the man who is to direct Ivan's education, the learned priest Makary, is no cloistered academic. Deeply immersed in the politics of his day, Makary is brought to the Kremlin when the saintly archbishop Joseph is exiled, an affair that provides Ivan with his first lesson in the relations between church and state in Russia. One morning before dawn, the solitary boy awakens to a strange sight: the archbishop is cowering next to his bed, begging for refuge. A few moments later the Shuiskys, the ruling power of the moment, break into the room with cries of rage. Their lackeys tear the old prelate's garments in a gesture of scorn, kicking and beating him to within an inch of his life while the young Ivan watches impassively and remains silent. His features betray not the slightest emotion.

From what Ivan says later on many occasions, we know that he suffered greatly during this time. He never forgets the horrors of his childhood, referring to them again and again. Even in the will he will write decades afterward, the details of his youth remain as fresh in his memory as if they had just occurred. But the boy who waits and watches the brutal goings-on day after day in the Kremlin appears indifferent. He has learned to wear a mask, to be a part of the spectacle even if that requires, for the moment, being passive.

Five years go by in this way. Ivan is thirteen, and thanks to his mentor, Archbishop Makary, he has immersed himself in the history of Byzantium and the ancient Russian state. His learning has given him a deeper sense of Russia's past and of her destiny. His isolation has made him thoughtful and a sharp observer. He is ready to test his wings.

The occasion is not long in coming. One of the minor nobility, a young man named Verontzov, befriends the lonely heir. The Shuisky family is in power again, and during one of the state councils, the head of the family, Andrei Shuisky, has words with Verontzov—because of some slight? because of his closeness to the heir? Shuisky needs no reason, since his power is at its height. Arrogantly, he and his cohort cover Verontzov with insults and send him into exile.

Ivan retreats in shame and sadness. He asks his mentor to intercede for his friend, but Makary has nothing to offer but his prayers. He counsels patience; perhaps the Belskys will once again seize power and reverse the Shuiskys' decision.

Three days later, Ivan appears as the great nobles feast. He is determined to assert his will, his resolve strengthened by Makary's teaching, by his own knowledge of where he should stand in the scheme of things. At the same time, he is conscious of the fact that he is taking an enormous risk, and that the desperate gamble will determine his entire future.

Silent, insignificant until this moment, the boy raises his voice with astonishing authority. "You have robbed and oppressed and dealt unjustly in the land," he begins, his phrases carefully chosen to have biblical resonance. "But I will forgive you," he continues, pausing to look at each one with a fearless gaze. "Only Shuisky cannot be spared." The nobles turn to each other with amazement—Shuisky is foremost among them! But there is something in the boy's voice, in his manner, that conveys authority, and he must be obeyed. Prince Shuisky is turned over to the royal hunters and put to death, his body thrown to the dogs.

Although four more years will pass until Ivan comes

into his own, the process has begun. By his strength of will, he has become a force to be reckoned with in the complicated power struggle of emerging Russia. From that day forward it is clear that he will be what he will name himself: Tsar.

III.   WOMB AND GRAVE

**The magic of first love is our ignorance that it
could ever end.**
　　　　　—Isaac d'Israeli

THE YEAR 1574. Two thousand young virgins and their
chaperones arrive at the Kremlin. Suites of rooms are
being prepared for the virgins, but not for the chaperones.
Rather, special women are assigned to keep watch during
the night; the girls, no matter how beautiful or intelligent,
will be sent home if they snore. No defect is insignificant,
no detail too small to notice! The Tsar, who is choosing his
fifth wife (in all, he will marry seven times), wants to set a
good example for his son, who will also select a mate from
this group.

　　Beauty is important to Ivan. He is a connoisseur. But
he advises his son not to be dazzled, as he himself was in
the choice of his second wife, a hastily converted barbarian
whom he married just eight days after the death of Anastasia—and whom he dismissed not long after—"divorce"
too formal a term to describe the way his marriages end.

　　"Character must be examined, intelligence, moral

purity," he instructs his son. "Sweetness of voice, manners, bodily health. . . ." He draws up a long list, conspicuously omitting lineage, normally a major consideration in the sixteenth century, especially in a royal marriage. However, in his choice of wives—and in his government appointments as well, his generals, councilors, and bishops—Ivan always puts individual value above pedigree. The wife he chooses on this occasion will be of merchant stock, although of course her family is raised to high honors the moment the marriage takes place.

Ivan goes to such lengths in preparing for marriage, but in a sense it is all a mockery. Anastasia is the only woman he will ever care about. He chooses his other wives for "bodily purposes," as he explains to the disapproving Church Council. The Church limits the number of wives to three, and an exception must be proclaimed for the Tsar. Given the number of women and girls Ivan sleeps with or rapes, it would seem that marriage should be irrelevant for him. But the *sacrament* of marriage retains a fascination for Ivan; there is a power and a blessing in the service, even though the marriage is loveless.

Anastasia was perfection, and there is no comparing his other wives with her. More than just a partner, she was an ideal for him to live up to. His marriage to her coincided with his assumption of power. A fire rages in Moscow just after the marriage is celebrated; a rumor begins that the corrupt and greedy Glinskys, the faction in power, started it. A riot takes place; Ivan restores order, banishes the Glinskys, and takes up the reins of government himself. He is seventeen and is ready to be proclaimed not only Grand Prince of Moscow, but also Tsar, Caesar. Russia will be a great empire in both Europe and Asia. Ivan's vision will allow him to accept no lesser raiment than the mantle of imperial Rome.

Under the influence of his bride, Anastasia, the new Tsar strives for both virtue and glory. Wanting to awaken the power of the great sleeping giant which is Russia, Ivan turns to wise counselors, the priest Sylvester and the low-born but clever Adashev. Major reforms follow; there are necessary changes in the structure of the government, which check the rapacity of the provincial governors and strengthen central authority. Ivan is at peace with himself; everything lies before him and his heart is filled with grat-itude. He makes a pilgrimage with Anastasia to give thanks, calmly, joyously, and to pray that his reign will be a glorious one.

It seems that his prayers are answered. He sets out to fight what will be his major military success: the taking of Kazan, a Tatar base of power. The war is a popular—more, a crucial—one. The Tatars have raided the Russian lands for centuries, demanding huge tributes and glutting the market in Istanbul with the vast numbers of Christians they have taken as slaves. The fighting is fierce, and al-though Ivan is never known for military prowess (he is, in fact, something of a coward and throughout the siege will remain for the most part in his tent), when he returns with his successful army, the nation proclaims him a hero.

All the church bells of Moscow peal; the streets are filled with his rejoicing subjects. Before the Kremlin, a purple cloak is draped over his shoulders, and his old men-tor, Makary, now archbishop, blesses him as Russia's savior. Anastasia is not present. She is not yet able to leave her bed, because during Ivan's absence she has borne him a son.

This is the pinnacle of Ivan's personal happiness. He has it all. He is secure in Anastasia's love; he rejoices over the birth of a son; he is beloved as a national hero; and he is surrounded by advisers whom he trusts, for Anastasia has

taught him to trust. The priest Sylvester and Ivan's favorite,
Adashev, head the chosen council, a small group of emi-
nently sane men, and while Ivan will not always accept
their advice, later calling their interference "intolerable,"
the truth is that the young Tsar needs such men around
him during his first years in power. They work well together, forging a new law code, reorganizing the army, and
even limiting the worldly power and wealth of the Church.

If this were an opera, we would hear dark chords at
this moment. For the fate inexorably awaiting Ivan and
Russia now appears on stage, in the form of a nearly fatal
illness. Ivan falls sick, and from day to day his condition
becomes worse. Feverish and weak, he calls the nobles to
the Kremlin to swear allegiance to his young son and wife
in the event of his death.

What is so painful is that the situation recalls his own
youth: his father Vasily III died in similar circumstances.
Suffering from a hunting wound that turned gangrenous,
Vasily had adjured the nobles to remain faithful to his infant son, Ivan, and Ivan's mother, Elena. But within five
years Elena was poisoned by jealous nobles, who plun-
dered the treasury, enslaved the powerless, and tore Russia
apart with coups and countercoups.

Now, as Ivan's condition becomes more and more serious, the great nobles and churchmen assemble in the
Kremlin to swear the oath Ivan requires. The churchman
Makary leads the loyal faction (as Ivan lies dying, factions
and parties begin to form). Surprisingly enough, those
closest to him, Sylvester and Adashev, now betray him.
Their motives are not greed or ambition; rather, they fear
the disorders that might erupt during a long regency. But
it is a betrayal nonetheless. They support the candidacy of
a cousin of Ivan's, a prince whose lineage gives him a good
claim to the throne. Such a man might prevent another

period of disorder and civil war; and yet it is understood that this would mean the probable murder of Ivan's infant son and the imprisonment of his widow in a convent.

With superhuman strength, shaking with fever and racked with pain, Ivan argues with the nobles. Reasoning with them, threatening, cursing, he imposes his will. One by one, they kiss the cross and on pain of eternal damnation, swear allegiance to the child.

And then Ivan astonishes everyone by recovering.

Here we encounter one of the great surprises of his reign. We would expect even the most mild-mannered ruler to take revenge on those whose loyalty wavered. But there is a radical disjuncture in Ivan's behavior, a pre-Anastasia, post-Anastasia split. The thirteen years of his marriage to Anastasia are an idyll during which his demons are kept at bay. And then, too, he has reenacted the death scene of his father and emerged triumphant. It is a moment of victory for him, and throughout his life, punishment will not depend on the guilt or innocence of Ivan's subjects but rather on the state of Ivan's soul: when he is tormented, he craves bloodshed; when he is at peace, even the guilty are set free.

Sylvester, Adashev, the royal cousin, the noble conspirators, all are spared. The crisis, however, reminds Ivan of the lessons of his youth. Though he forgives them, the seeds of distrust and hatred are sown.

But this is a time for rejoicing. As soon as he is able, Ivan takes Anastasia and their newborn child on a pilgrimage to the Kirilov monastery far to the north. Everyone pleads with him to put off the trip, a long and arduous one in the middle of winter. But years before, his mother had taken the same pilgrimage in fulfillment of a vow made when she was pregnant with Ivan. The mock death scene he had played out connected Ivan with his father, and now an obscure instinct drives him back to the place where he was blessed in the womb.

Solemnly, as if anticipating what will happen, Ivan arrives in Kirilov as a humble penitent. He disembarks from the riverboat and walks to the monastery barefoot in the snow. But the shadow of death has not yet withdrawn from the royal household. As the young Tsar offers up thanks for his own deliverance, his firstborn son dies.

IV.   RAW MEAT

Answer a fool according to his folly.
—Proverbs 26, Verse 5

THE YEAR 1570. A humble shed on the outskirts of the great Russian city, Pskov. It is overrun with wounded animals, some blind, some half starved. There are birds with broken wings, crippled dogs, and hundreds of stray cats, all tended by a lean, taciturn figure known as Crazy Nicholashka, or Nicholas the Hermit. He is not a member of any monastic order but, like the animals he tends, is a "stray," a "holy fool," one of the half-crazed ascetics held in great veneration by the common people and even by the nobility.

For days he has been seen wandering in the woods, half naked and crying out incoherently as if he were in great pain, although there is no apparent reason for his agitation. Later it will be said that he received a prophetic vision of the evil threatening the city. Of course, there is no way of telling what he "saw," but certainly by the time Ivan arrives in Pskov, the tragedy that has just taken place in the neighboring city of Novgorod is known far and wide. Ivan has attacked Novgorod—along with Moscow, the greatest city in his empire—as if it belonged to an enemy. To make sure of surprising the population, an advance guard had preceded him on the road to Novgorod, murdering any travelers they met. A barricade was thrown up and the great destruction began.

Methodically, *oprichniki* went from house to house, slitting throats, raping and looting. Day after day, victims drawn from every class, poor peasants, rich merchants, priests, nobles, men, women, and children, were herded together for the spectacle of public torture commanded by the Tsar.

Although mutiny was given as the reason for the massacre, it was merely a pretext. A criminal punished in Novgorod had denounced the city, claiming that a treasonous letter to the Polish king was hidden in the cathedral. The letter was produced, an obvious forgery, and the Tsar arrived in Novgorod, to find the bishop and nobles gathered to welcome him with awe.

But the sight of his submissive subjects instead of calming his rage increased it. Year by year since Anastasia's death, Ivan has been giving himself up to his instinct for cruelty and now he is ready for the final chapter of his reign. He never surpassed the magnitude of his crimes in Novgorod, both for sheer numbers and for fiendish refinement of cruelty. An entire city perished at his nod.

The tortures were endlessly prolonged. Victims were castrated, impaled through rectum and neck, or submerged in freezing then boiling water. Death, when it came, was welcomed as a grace. Yet an astonishing phenomenon occurred: with mutilated features and broken limbs, many died praying for the Tsar. Such is the mystical power of his sway over them. Similarly, centuries later many of those imprisoned under Stalin will give way to frantic grief when hearing of his death.

Novgorod has been humbled. A small remnant of pitiful survivors, many driven insane by what they have seen, gathered in the square to bid farewell to the Tsar who has left these witnesses to his power. "You have been pardoned," he tells them, though their only crime was to have lived in the city. "Pray for my welfare." And heading for Pskov, he galloped out of Novgorod through silent streets filled with the insane and the dead.

Pskov is his next goal in this war against his own people. Perhaps it is significant that these two cities are chosen. Both are centers of wealth, trade, and culture, with histories that predate Moscow's. Both have memories of independence, their subjection to Moscow going back only two generations. They lie near the western border, that is, near the territory of Ivan's enemy the king of Poland. And intermittently, there has been some unrest in both; they have petitioned the Tsar for the redress of grievances.

In the past, Ivan's father and grandfather alternated between force and negotiation when dealing with the citizens of Novgorod—called "Novgorod the Great"— confirming their special privileges while drawing them into the empire. But Ivan settles the case once and for all in a way that only his unbridled savagery can. The city is crushed so thoroughly that it will never recover its former significance; Moscow's supremacy is confirmed, never again to be challenged.

Riding at the head of his army, Ivan reaches Pskov. His unarmed subjects kneel in the snow, the nobles welcome him with traditional platters of bread and salt, the bishop receives him with blessings. He retires to rest in a monastery and the city awaits its fate. Church bells toll all night while the population observes a vigil of fasting and prayer.

And then the miracle.

Before starting the slaughter, Ivan decides to visit a holy fool he has heard about, Nicholas the Hermit, and ask for his blessing. But as he approaches the shed, a loud voice cries out, telling the Tsar to go away.

Ivan orders the door broken down, then steps inside the small hut filled with animals and crude crosses. The half-starved Nicholas, dressed in rags, steps forward boldly and thrusts a chunk of raw meat into the Tsar's hands.

"I don't eat meat during Lent," Ivan says, not taken aback by the "gift" but entering naturally into the madman's world. Bishops and priests may be thrown to the bears, but in a way, Ivan and the holy fool are kindred spirits.

"You do worse! You drink the blood of Christians," Nicholas answers him. "But touch a hair on the head of the least child in this city, and God will strike you dead."

As he speaks the sky darkens, and Ivan backs away. Orders are given for the army to retreat. Pskov is left unharmed, and Nicholas, unaware that he is made a saint by the grateful city, returns to his wounded animals and his prayers.

V. THE THREE PETTICOATS

As a madman who casteth firebrands, arrows and death, and sayeth to his neighbor, "Am I not in jest?"

Proverbs 26, verse 18

THE YEAR 1581. A feast is in progress, the dining hall tables replete with a profusion of exotic foods, everything from stuffed ostrich eggs to elks' brains, washed down with Malmsey, kvass, and vodka by the barrel. Obscene buffoons provide the merriment, and the Tsar himself dons a mask and dances with abandon. But there is no reason for celebration.

Just the opposite. There is reason for concern and worry, since a vigorous new king, Stephen Báthory, has been chosen for the throne of Poland on the death of Ivan's old adversary, Sigismund Augustus. Ivan had tried to convince the Polish nobility, who elect their sovereign, that he himself would be the best choice, imagining that he would then combine the Russian and Polish kingdoms and achieve through diplomacy what he had been trying to win in war, the conquest of Livonia. In an effort to rehabilitate his reputation, he goes so far as to disband the *oprichniki,* an act of "public relations" he hopes will impress Europe. But numerous pamphlets and letters describing his brutality have been circulated throughout the continent, and refugees from his terror provide firsthand accounts. Stephen Báthory is elected and immediately challenges Ivan, calling him a coward. Báthory knows that although the Tsar will lead an army against his own defenseless subjects, he never risks his safety in combat.

Báthory is remarkably successful in war, taking city after city in Russian-occupied Livonia. The importance of these lands on the Baltic cannot be overestimated for Russia's development. It's not simply a question of breaking the embargo on the new military technology from the West, an embargo which at different points Denmark, Sweden, and Poland try to enforce; a port on the Baltic would increase Russia's participation in the life and politics of western Europe. Ivan's attempt to obtain a "window on the West" for Russia results in a war that lasts intermittently for twenty-five years. But while his victories over the Tatars will be permanent, the successes he achieves in Livonia at the beginning of his reign are reversed by the end, and it will be up to Peter the Great to complete his work.

The Tsar chooses to take no notice of Báthory's victories, however. The banquet continues, and if the Tsar jokes a little too roughly with one of his companions by pouring a cauldron of scalding soup over his head, still, it is only in jest. A doctor is called and commanded to revive the man, but he is past saving and the feast goes on with a ribald toast to the deceased.

The heir is not present, a fact Ivan notices with impatience. A young man of twenty-seven, the Tsarevitch has become his father's companion in debauchery and torture, proving his devotion by saving Ivan's life when a shackled prisoner gets loose one day and tries to kill the Tsar. Quick as an arrow, the Tsarevitch lunges forward and cuts the would-be assassin down, sealing the bond between him and his father in blood.

But of late there has been some strain between them. The young man has dreams of military glory and begs that his father allow him to answer Báthory's taunts. Ivan refuses, since he knows how difficult it will be to face the Polish king at this point in his reign: for hundreds of miles around Moscow, the peasants have fled from Ivan's harsh rule; the great estates have been devastated by his followers; and the leading generals have been killed on his orders. Adding to the Tsar's displeasure is the fact that by coincidence a delegation has arrived asking the Tsar to appoint his son to lead the troops. And while the Tsarevitch swears that he has had nothing to do with this, his father's suspicions are aroused.

Leaning on his iron-tipped staff, Ivan rises slowly from his heavy feasting and makes his way to a chapel to pray. But no sooner does he turn to the silver and gold icons than the Tsarevitch bursts in demanding an explanation. At first Ivan looks at him with heavy eyes. He dislikes being interrupted at his prayers. But his annoyance quickly turns to fury when the Tsarevitch starts to reproach him. Is it for the son to chastise the father? That morning, coming upon his daughter-in-law wearing only one petticoat, and not three, as befits the wife of the heir, he struck her, perhaps beat her, what does it matter? There have been so many dead, so many tortured, that Ivan barely takes in the news that his pregnant daughter-in-law has miscarried.

But the Tsarevitch's tone—*that* he does take in. The boy is insolent and dares to raise his voice to God's anointed! Ivan strikes him again and again with his irontipped staff. Only as the young man crumples to the ground does the father rush forward to cradle his son in his arms, crying out for help and begging for forgiveness.

The son lingers for three days, during which time the father neither eats nor sleeps but stands weeping before the icons, imploring God to be merciful. On the third day, toward evening, Ivan sees that the doctors have stopped whispering among themselves. Approaching the bed, he falls on his son in despair. The Tsarevitch is dead.

During the last years of his life, Ivan goes in for a strange sort of bookkeeping. He wanders through the Kremlin desperately trying to remember the names of his victims. Drawing up lists that are sometimes quite detailed but at other times are only vague memories, he might scrawl "A hundred families in a small village near Moscow" or "Thirty brothers in a monastery in Pskov." Or he might record "the Prince Vasily Staritsky, his wife and two children," and include a date and place. The lists of the victims are sent to monasteries along with large gifts of gold, so that the monks might pray for their souls.

He makes peace with Báthory, giving up all claim to Livonia.

Almost by accident, a band of convict-adventurers conquers a huge addition to the Russian empire, Siberia. Ivan hardly notices. He composes a hymn to Death.

A young woman bears him another son, Dmitri, but this child is destined never to rule, or rather to rule only in a ghostly way. Dmitri will be murdered in his youth by Ivan's successor Fyodor's regent Boris Godunov—and will be resurrected twice by pretenders to the throne, two false Dmitris who claim to be the murdered child. And so, with Ivan, the seven-hundred-year-old dynasty of Rurik comes to an end.

During his last days, Ivan suffers horribly in body and spirit. Sometimes he will call out to his son in the middle of state business and hold a conversation with the murdered Tsarevitch. Ivan's stomach and genitals swell grotesquely and he takes to his bed, calling for astrologers and necromancers to predict his fate. He is told that he will die on March 18, and when the day comes, he sends word that he will have these false prophets killed. "The day is not yet over," they reply, and the fact is that they are right. Ivan comes out of his bath and calls for his chessboard. But before he can begin the game, he falls forward onto his bed, his fierce eyes still hypnotic, as if he were trying to command just one more death to appease his rage and sorrow.

POSTSCRIPT

Under Stalin, during repairs to the Cathedral of St. Michael the Archangel, Ivan's tomb is opened and his skull and bones are X-rayed. Nothing of scientific interest is discovered, although a sculptor will use the skull as a model when casting a bronze statue of the Tsar. Ivan's shroud has long since crumbled to dust. It would have been a simple monk's robe; he had requested that the service be read over his dead body and that he be anointed with sacred oil and buried as a monk.

A jar of Venetian glass is also found in the tomb. When it is opened the workers are surprised to find that the unused oil has not evaporated. Perhaps Ivan has left it for those who will follow him. They too will have great need of forgiveness.

HITLER

I. A SPECIAL DELIVERY

That a poor little creature had to be killed to make your meal!
> —Adolf Hitler, a vegetarian (watching
> a table companion eat veal)

PARIS, 1940. A swastika flutters from the Eiffel Tower in the heart of the occupied city. Not far away, a military car pulls up in front of an elegant building. Two SS men jump out, push aside the concierge, and go inside. Shortly afterward, they emerge carrying a package, which is rushed to Berlin by special courier. Wherever the courier is stopped, a few whispered words produce an immediate effect—he is sped on his way until he reaches the Chancellery, where Hitler is waiting.

Without a word, the package is delivered to Christa Schroeder, one of his secretaries, who immediately calls the Führer's intimates to tell them the news: it has arrived.

Not long afterward, they appear at the grandiosely re-built Chancellery. A veritable *Who's Who* of Nazi Germany, one by one they walk up the marble steps and into the vast entranceway past the gigantic statues of rearing stallions and the two nude, uncircumcised men who symbolize the Party and the new German army of the impotent Hitler.

First to make his appearance is the twisted yet brilliant minister of propaganda, Joseph Goebbels, the "Little Doctor" as he is known. A failed novelist and academic, clubfooted and oversexed, he is Hitler's man, body and soul. Only when he tries to leave his wife for a Czech actress does he fall out of favor; Hitler admires his wife, Magda, and orders Goebbels back to her bed.

Next comes the obese Hermann Göring, Hitler's chosen successor, sporting a field marshal's baton covered with jewels and wearing a sable coat. Once a daredevil pilot in World War I, now he is the pleasure-loving and drug-addicted Commander-in-Chief of the Air Force, Plenipotentiary of the Four-Year Plan, etc., etc. His long list of grandiose titles satisfies even his enormous vanity, but in fact he does very little work. In the early days of the Party, his main use to the Führer was a social one. At home in upper-class circles, he cut a dashing figure in society, helping put Hitler in touch with major industrialists, among them Fritz Thyssen, the steel magnate whose contributions will be crucial to the Party's success. As head of the air force, Göring now spends his time hunting and gorging himself on exotic foods—when he is not looting the museums of Europe for art treasures to adorn his magnificent estate, Karinhall. In contrast to Hitler's preference for simplicity, Göring dresses in a variety of splashy uniforms, which he spends hours designing. The successes of the air force are achieved despite him, while its failures are a direct result of his arrogance and sloth and drugged trances. Unrepentant, at Nuremberg he will tell his lawyer to limit his defense to three words: "Lick my ass!"

The foreign minister, Joachim von Ribbentrop, an old

enemy of Göring's, also shows up at this gathering of the inner circle. He is foolish, pretentious, monocled. At first Hitler's ambassador to Great Britain, he advises Hitler to invade Poland despite England's threats. England will never go to war, he says with confidence. An ex-champagne salesman whose ennobling "von" is spurious, he is a good example of what Mussolini's son-in-law Ciano has called the Third Reich leaders: "Gangsters who have married wealth"—a description that also happens to fit Ciano himself.

Then there is Heinrich Himmler, head of the gestapo and one of the darkest figures in the Third Reich. An ex-chicken farmer, now he is entrusted with the lives of millions of the conquered, whom Hitler will enslave and murder. Hitler has put Himmler in charge of the "final solution" of the Jewish problem as well as of the sadistic "experiments" conducted on thousands of "subhumans," that is, Jews, Poles, Russians, Ukrainians, Gypsies, Communists, homosexuals, Jehovah's Witnesses, intellectuals, and other dissenters and undesirables. He is a passionless automaton, the bureaucrat par excellence, only the reports he writes include statistics like "40,000 Jews deported," and "10,000 Russian prisoners defleshed for our skeletal studies," etc. When his own nephew is discovered to be a homosexual, he allows him to die in one of his concentration camps rather than break the rules. Above all, procedure must be followed.

And last of all is Albert Speer, the most thoughtful of the crew, whose intelligence makes his guilt all the greater. An architect, he is seduced by the possibilities and power Hitler holds out to him; Berlin, Munich, all of Germany will need to be rebuilt on a grander scale after the war. He is in charge of armaments production, and achieves miracles in increasing Germany's output, right to the end, despite heavy Allied bombing. He achieves these results partly because of his genius for organization, partly because of his unscrupulous use of slave labor. Thousands of men and women are worked to death in his arms factories.

They await the Führer in silence, for there is jealousy and enmity between them, encouraged by Hitler, who thus strengthens his power over them.

They have not long to wait. Hitler has come straight back to the Chancellery on hearing that a messenger has brought the precious package. Bormann, Hitler's sinister and conniving personal secretary, throws open the door and announces, "The Führer," as everyone rises and salutes.

The Führer's face is pasty, his expression dreamy. He takes quick, mincing steps. His "womanish" gestures and stride frequently surprise those who meet him for the first time. In public, he carefully contrives every stance to express hypermasculine power; when he is relaxed, however, he frequently lapses into a grotesque parody of femininity. But if he unconsciously parodies femininity, his idea of the masculine is no less a parody, bound up as it is with brutality and aggression. Especially when talking to women, he ridiculously imitates his notion of the "superman," flourishing a rhino-hide whip and shouting orders at his dog.

The fact is that Hitler is neither homosexual nor truly heterosexual, regardless of the nature of his relationships with women. The best definition of his sexuality is the one given by Helene Hanfstaengl, the wife of his foreign press secretary. She has known Hitler well from the early days of the Party and on one occasion is even the object of his "desire." On a visit to her home, he falls to his knees and moans about his tragic love for her while her husband is out of the room. It is an avowal she does not take seriously, because it is obvious to her that he is "a neuter." His libido is bound up with his politics, and his truly orgiastic moments occur during his speeches, their savage climaxes achieved amidst roaring, ecstatic crowds. "Politics is like a woman," he is given to saying. "If you don't love her properly she will bite your head off."

"Gentlemen, be seated," Hitler says in a low voice. He is tired and sends for his doctor, Theodor Morell, who is always on hand with an injection of stimulants. It has been a long day of meetings, ending in a public appearance to present "Hero-Mother" medals, prizes awarded to women who have produced five or more children for the Fatherland. Although the aim of increasing the population is a political one, the prizes also reflect Hitler's obsession with motherhood. Photos of his own mother are to be found at all of his residences, and an early, sentimental poem about Mother's Day by Hitler is published in a Munich newspaper, adjuring the readers to remember their mothers when they are old and in failing health.

Hitler's rhapsodies on motherhood are in keeping with his general sentimentality, the cloying sweetness which is the brutal dictator's other side. He makes up for his lack of real human feeling by falsely displaying emotion, and it is this pretense of feeling which is at the root of his sentimentality.

But real or imagined, Hitler's emotions about such matters are not to be trifled with. Frau Rascher, a clever opportunist, personifies an ironic example of Hitler's touchiness on his sacred subjects. Her husband, Dr. Rascher, is in charge of the freezing and high-altitude experiments at Dachau, experiments that will supposedly be of use to the air force if pilots are shot down in arctic waters or if their planes are strafed by enemy fire. In actuality, the scientific value of these experiments is nil, Nazi

"science" being profoundly out of touch with reality.
Naked concentration camp inmates are left for hours in
vats of freezing water while Rascher charts their temper-
atures and the length of time it takes for them to die.
Other victims are put into special decompression chambers and "data" similarly recorded. At Nuremberg a witness will testify: "I have watched through the observation
window of the decompression chamber when a prisoner
inside would stand in a vacuum until his lungs rupture.
They would go mad and pull out their hair in an effort to
relieve the pressure. They would tear their heads and face
with their fingers and nails in an attempt to maim themselves in their madness. They would beat the walls with
their hands and head and scream in an effort to relieve
pressure on their eardrums. Their agony would finally end
in death."

Dr. Rascher's experiments impress the Nazi hierarchy,
but the fact that he and his wife have no children is a mark
against him in the insane world of the Third Reich.
Certain promotions are not within his grasp. The Lady
Macbeth–like Frau Rascher, who is as cruel as her husband—she has been known to beat her household slaves,
recruited from the camps, to death—urges her husband to
perpetrate a hoax. Although she is forty-eight years old,
she pretends to have given birth to a child. The infant, of
course, is one that has been kidnapped from a state orphanage. The hoax is a success and she is held up as a wonder of German motherhood and Nazi science, which has
enabled her to bear children at such a late age. A second
and then a third child follow.

But the honors awarded Frau Rascher will lead to her
downfall. Frau Rascher is named a "Hero Mother," and
Dr. Rascher is honored for his scientific work. Honor
brings jealousy with it, and a rival doctor does some

sleuthing. It is not long before an orphanage nurse is found who will report the fraud to the authorities. The Raschers' bestial cruelty, commendable from the Nazi point of view, is not enough to save them from paying for this outrage, this slur on glorious German motherhood. The couple is marched before a firing squad and executed, Frau Rascher's cries for mercy going unheeded.

Experiments continue, with other doctors in charge (some quite distinguished in their fields, such as Edwin Katzenellenbogen, formerly on the Harvard medical faculty): experiments in sterilization, gangrene, any topic the doctors' fiendish imaginations are capable of. It is this kind of cruelty that gives the lie to Hitler's sentimental poses, when he praises motherhood, or goes into raptures over favorite actress Shirley Temple, or plays at being "Uncle Adolf" with Goebbels's seven children and Bormann's ten. His sentimentality, his excess of feeling—false feeling, really—at these moments is the other side of his lack of feeling at other times. It is a case of *les extremes touchant,* of seeming opposites actually being the same.

Now, surrounded by his cronies, fortified by an injection from Dr. Morell, a plate of sweets before him, Hitler gives the order, "Let us begin."

The package delivered from Paris is brought in by the secretary. A screen is lowered, lights dim, and a movie projector starts to roll as the Nazi hierarchy watches in rapt attention.

War, war, war—all you men ever talk about is war! Scarlett O'Hara simpers, sitting on the steps of a Southern plantation. Dr. Schmidt, Hitler's official translator, repeats in German Scarlett's complaint, simper and all. Up until the fall of Paris, it had not been possible to obtain reels of the forbidden film, produced by Jews, from Metro-Goldwyn-Mayer. Now it is a comparatively simple matter to raid the

MGM safe in Paris and bring the Old South of *Gone With the Wind* to Berlin.

Hitler's absorption in the movie is more than a tribute to Hollywood. It is an indication of how much in the Third Reich is based on fantasy and theatricality.

Simply in terms of surroundings, the rebuilt Chancellery in Berlin, with its immense chambers and marble columns, and the Berghof, Hitler's spectacular Alpine retreat, are like magnificent stage sets meant to produce an effect on those who traverse their vast spaces.

When the Austrian chancellor Schuschnigg comes to negotiate with Hitler in the Alps, first he must drive for ten miles around hairpin curves up the side of a mountain. Then he is made to walk through an underground passage and must ascend some seven hundred feet in an elevator built inside of the mountain peak. Stepping out into a gallery of Greek pillars, the chancellor finds himself in an enormous high-ceilinged hall with glass walls looking out over mountains stretching in every direction. The view from the Berghof is dizzying, hallucinatory, the effect on Schuschnigg that of hanging in midair. There, dressed in his storm trooper uniform, Hitler awaits him.

Before Schuschnigg can finish his greeting, the Führer shocks him by cutting him off in a hoarse, contemptuous voice. The Austrian chancellor, used to the polite language of diplomacy, is further thrown off balance by the coarse threats hurled at him, by the intimidating presence of the Nazi generals, by the primal hatred flashing in Hitler's eyes, by his ferocity. Everything in the Führer's hysterical, hate-crazed attitude indicates that he is not only *willing* to go to war, but that he lives only for conquest.

There is no question that to a certain extent Hitler's

fury is genuine; he has endless reserves of hatred to draw on. How much of this is theater, however, can be seen after he sends Schuschnigg to wait in an anteroom while he confers with his chief of staff, General Keitel. Chief of the OKW, the High Command of the Armed Forces, this lackey will later be hanged at Nuremberg.

When the general asks why he has been summoned, Hitler answers "For no reason," and laughs maliciously. It has been part of the show he's put on to break Schuschnigg. Not only in this instance, but in all his negotiations, Hitler calculates the effect he is producing like a masterful performer. Very few of his victims have the stamina to hold their own in such circumstances.

Schuschnigg certainly does not. That day, he is bullied into signing an agreement which compromises Austria's independence. Within a week, Austria will be completely absorbed into the Reich, and within a year Schuschnigg himself will be imprisoned in a concentration camp, scrubbing the floors of the latrines with a toothbrush as SS guards jeer at him.

But Hitler can use his histrionic gifts to inspire as well as to terrify. Especially after the tide of war begins to turn against Germany, officers will arrive at headquarters determined to tell the Führer that the war is lost, only to lose their nerve under his hypnotic gaze. Under orders to deliver pessimistic messages, they remain silent in the Führer's presence, and return to battle ready to die for a cause which they now know will be victorious—because their Führer has said it will be so.

To what extent Hitler loses himself in his role and to what extent he stands apart from it, an observer of his own actions, is sometimes difficult to know; he himself at times must be unsure.

Both of these elements, passion and calculation, are

significant in the 1934 purge of the Nazi Party. Hitler carries out the purge against his own most fanatical followers, the SA Brownshirts, a paramilitary organization which has been the muscle of the Nazi Party. Ten years earlier, Hitler had led these same Brownshirts in an attempt to overthrow the state, a failed putsch for which he spent a year in jail. But since then he has focused on a "legal" takeover, trying to win seats for the Nazi Party in the national elections. His idea is to overthrow the Republic from within, rising to power through the normal channels and then turning that limited power into absolute power.

At first the Nazis aren't able to win a majority of seats in the Reichstag (later on, only 5 percent of the population won't vote for them). Even without a majority, however, Hitler manages to be appointed chancellor in a coalition government, though his hold on power is shaky. The economic position of post–World War I Germany is desperate, and a series of short-lived coalitions has preceded the one that put Hitler in power. One chancellor after another has tried to rule but each has been quickly forced out, defeated by the political chaos. For with Germany's defeat in World War I and the abdication of the kaiser, more than a dozen political parties try to rule the fragmented Republic, each party at cross-purposes with the other. Only the monolithic army remains a significant force in Germany's political life, but the army is hostile to democracy and hopes for the return of autocratic rule.

As chancellor, Hitler now faces a difficult choice: he is caught between the army and his followers. The SA Brownshirts, led by the brutal, scar-faced Ernst Röhm, want a "Nazi revolution" that turns Germany upside down, with key positions going to radical Nazis. Ever since Hitler's appointment, his SA followers have acted like lords of the land, roaring through the streets in their SA cars and beating up whomever they like while Röhm scandalizes the army with his open homosexuality, surrounding himself with a coterie of young men and sending his SA pimps throughout Germany to find lovers.

During the Third Reich, thousands of gays are condemned to concentration camps; they are more relentlessly persecuted by the Nazis than at any other time in Germany's history. Therefore, it is a measure of Hitler's regard for Röhm that he ignores his homosexuality, finding in the SA leader a kindred spirit, violent, filled with hatred, prepared to do anything to achieve his ends, an ardent believer in Nazi doctrine. He dismisses Röhm's sexual preference as a result of "time spent in the tropics." On the subject of the homosexuality of two of his heroes, Frederick the Great of Prussia and Wagner's patron King Ludwig of Bavaria, Hitler is silent.

The conservative, aristocratic army generals will only support Hitler's regime if he turns against the rabble surrounding him, the SA Brownshirts, who have been with the Führer through his lean days when the Party was illegal, and Röhm, who served a prison sentence with Hitler for their part in the failed 1923 putsch. The army wants to preserve its privilege as the only bearer of arms in the state; they want the SA disbanded. Röhm and the other SA leaders want to be given key positions of control over the army. And Hitler wants to destroy the Republic and rule as absolute dictator.

Calculating which way the road to power lies, Hitler sides against his own followers and with the generals. Without warning, he swoops down on hundreds of SA Brownshirts in a bloodbath the Nazis will call the Night of the Long Knives. Accused of treason, the SA leaders are dragged out of bed, arrested in beer halls, surrounded in their barracks, and, in one case, interrupted in the midst of a honeymoon to be immediately shot, without trial, without explanation. They die with the cry *Heil Hitler!* on their lips, deluded to the last.

Hitler personally drives out to the country to arrest Röhm, who is staying with a group of SA officers and their boyfriends at an inn called the Hanslbauer, Little Hansel's House. One of them, Ernst Heines, the head of the SA in Silesia, a huge, baby-faced man with a wrestler's body, refuses to get dressed, until Hitler threatens to shoot him on the spot. The Führer has been conflicted up to this very moment; it is difficult for him to turn on Röhm, whose many services to the Nazi Party have been crucial and who has risked his life more than once for Hitler. Although Hitler has wanted merely to imprison Röhm, Göring and Goebbels have argued with Hitler that he cannot destroy the SA without killing its leader. And now, at the moment of truth, Hitler goes into a hysterical tirade, shrieking, "Treason! Traitors! Enemies of Germany!" and ordering his bodyguard to arrest everyone in the Hanslbauer. As a special favor, Röhm will be given the choice of suicide or execution. He says, "If Adolf wants to kill me, he will have to do it himself," and is shot to death by the bodyguard, his last words *"Mein Führer, mein Führer,"* as he bleeds to death on the floor.

To justify these massive arrests, this unprecedented slaughter in peacetime Germany, of not only SA chiefs but political enemies and even private individuals who simply "know too much," the Führer addresses the nation in a radio broadcast. Claiming that there was no time to worry about legal procedures because the danger was too great, he delivers a passionate speech to condemn the immoral traitors who have endangered Germany's welfare. Even today, it is impossible to listen to recordings of this speech without being impressed by Hitler's seeming sincerity and feeling. Even today, it takes a conscious effort not to be seduced by the voice, which sounds so heartbroken at the treachery of these "old fighters" for his cause. The Reichstag retroactively sanctions the illegal acts; the nation agrees with their Führer. And this is the beginning of the end, the suspension in the Third Reich of any law but Hitler's will.

Even the generals, who now throw in their lot with the Führer, will soon understand with whom they have made a bargain. Long an independent and privileged caste, the army will succumb to Hitler's "Nazification" process over the next two years. Preparing for war—*his* kind of war, not theirs, a reckless adventure that ignores any prudent, strategic considerations and eventually ignores reality—Hitler now purges the army of its "reactionary" elements.

First he gets rid of Commander in Chief Blomberg on a pretext; next he discredits von Fritsch, the man chosen by the army to succeed Blomberg by coercing a male prostitute into making false charges. Finally taking control of the army himself, Hitler cashiers everyone and anyone who refuses to acknowledge his absolute supremacy and genius. Going back on his promise that the army will be the only institution to bear arms, Hitler raises up the SS to replace the destroyed SA, and SS divisions of the army are created (the *SS Wehrmacht*). Thus the generals, who have thought to make Hitler into their tool, find themselves enslaved by a man who despises them. For better or worse, World War II will be Hitler's war; the generals will either be reduced to errand boys or will find themselves on forced leave. Hitler will brook no opposition.

In his conduct of the war, fantasy is more important for the Führer than strategy or historical examples. Noble poses. Theatrical gestures. The same factor that makes

Hitler's speeches so effective is his own belief in his performance—at least while he is giving it. His ability to lose
himself in fantasy is the key to understanding his decisions
during the war. Because although Hitler has read the great
tactician Clausewitz and knows the battle plans of World
War I by heart, if a single text had to be named as being
the most influential, it would be the tales of America's
Wild West he read as a boy. And not only as a boy. Egon
Hanfstaengl, the twelve-year-old son of Hitler's foreign
press secretary, is surprised to see the bookshelves in
Hitler's bedroom filled with these stories of Indian cunning and pioneer bravery, tales which Egon himself has already outgrown. On many occasions when the generals,
weighed down by the responsibility for hundreds of thousands of young lives, try to talk Hitler out of a plan they
consider too risky, Hitler's response is to wish they had
more of the Wild West in them. He is a boy playing a
game.

In the campaign against France, the Führer's bravado
pays off. Sending his panzer troops through hilly terrain
unsuitable for tank warfare, he attacks the Allies where
they least expect it and overwhelms France in six weeks,
almost capturing the entire British expeditionary force as
well (evacuated at Dunkirk in the nick of time).

But when Hitler turns on Russia he loses his reckless,
all-or-nothing gamble. The campaign against Russia has all
the treachery of an Indian ambush as Hitler imagined one.
Barely two years before, the Führer had signed a pact with
Stalin promising peace and cooperation. The arrangement
between the two countries was a marriage of convenience: it gave Hitler the freedom to fight Britain without
having to worry about his eastern front, and Stalin got
time to push Russia toward military readiness. Of course,
Stalin realizes that sooner or later the two countries will

come to war. But for all his distrust of "that hysteric Hitler," as he calls him, the Russian leader never dreams that war will come so soon. He is awakened in the middle of the night to hear the news that hundreds of thousands of German troops have crossed the border. Stalin is speechless with astonishment, as Hitler calculated he would be.

At first the German armies advance rapidly through Russia, which collapses like a house of cards. With Leningrad besieged and German troops camped forty miles outside of Moscow, Stalingrad becomes the turning point of the Russian campaign. The city is contested in desperate fighting, block by block, house by house, with enormous losses on both sides. At first the Germans capture the railway station in the heart of the city and for a time even manage to cut the Russian line of communication, pushing forward toward the river. Russian soldiers flee in panic; there are long lines of refugees strafed by German planes; whole army groups disintegrate in confusion; Soviet generals lead the exodus from the burning city in armored vehicles.

But Stalin rushes reinforcements to the beleaguered defenders, making it clear that the city bearing his name will not fall. As summer gives way to fall, and fall to winter, which comes early this year, with record-breaking cold, the tide turns. When fresh Soviet divisions, their existence unsuspected by Hitler, threaten to encircle the German Sixth Army, its commander, General Paulus, begs the Führer for permission to retreat.

But Hitler has always rejected the idea of strategic retreat. Of course the 300,000-man army can save its life by pulling back to fight another day (as the British have done at Dunkirk). But no. "Victory or death!" Hitler insists, with a deluded, schoolboy romanticism straight out of the Wild

West romances of his youth. "Where the German soldier has set his foot, he must never retreat!" The bitterness between him and his generals, who can not bear to watch the costly lunacy of Hitler's tactics, becomes so intense that the Führer refuses to eat with or shake the hands of any of the men on his staff.

The news gets worse and worse: troops encircled; almost no fuel or ammunition left; isolated groups of soldiers surrendering; awful sanitary conditions; men suffering from frostbite, hunger, dysentery, and so on, an appalling litany of disaster. An airlift gets scanty supplies through, not nearly enough.

From his vacation home in sunny Italy, Göring broadcasts a Christmas message for the men of Stalingrad that echoes his Führer: "Your bravery will be eternally celebrated in history!"

Permission is requested to attempt a "breakout," but Hitler refuses, countering with the order that the troops make a hedgehog formation and fight to the last man. To encourage heroism in their last hour, he jumps all the officers a rank and awards Paulus a field marshal's baton. "There is no record of a German field marshal ever having surrendered," he reasons. "Let their bravery be a shining example to all Germans."

With Beethoven's Fifth Symphony playing in the background, the nation hears the news: 300,000 dead, 91,000 captured. Of the captured, only 5,000 will return from the Russian prison camps at the end of the war.

It is a spectacular defeat, a defeat sown in the seeds of the first intoxicating victories, which made Hitler feel infallible. The line between fantasy and reality was lost as Germany either defeated or drew into its orbit Italy, Czechoslovakia, Austria, Poland, France, Norway, Hungary, Yugoslavia, Romania, Hungary, Belgium, Holland, Denmark, and Greece. His conquests were fantastic, almost unimaginable; a new page, a new chapter, a new volume had been written in history. How could he have dreamed that in just a few years the Third Reich would be no more, with Berlin in ruins, his chancellery a heap of rubble? The very Mercedes he rode through Berlin that day will end up in an amusement park in the United States, with thrill-seekers paying for the chance to sit "where that monster of depravity, Adolf Hitler, once sat!" as the barker intones. "Yes, ladies and gentlemen, just two bits! *This* was his car!"

But in 1940, all of this is still in the future. In 1940, Hitler and his henchmen sit drinking sweet tea and discussing *Gone With the Wind,* a movie they have found very satisfying. The meeting goes on till late at night, because the Führer is an insomniac who has a horror of being alone until he falls into bed, exhausted. Thus it is not until dawn begins to break over Berlin that one by one they take their leave: Göring, Goebbels, Speer, Bormann, Ribbentrop, and Himmler. They march down the marble staircase with the arrogance of power, each an actor in the Führer's *Third Reich,* each unaware that there will be a surprise ending. For with the exception of Speer (who will serve a life sentence), in less than five years each of the others, by his own hand or a Russian bomb or the hangman's noose, will be dead.

II.   IN THE BUNKER: ORDERS FOR DEAD MEN

At that moment I was reborn! Now I knew which road to take. This was a command!
—Joseph Goebbels, hearing Hitler
speak for the first time in Munich

APRIL 1945, BERLIN. The "Führer bunker." It is the very end. Suddenly manic laughter and partying have begun even among the most faithful of the faithful. Hitler's secretaries, adjutants, valets, cooks, and various liaison officers are gathered to make a last stand with their Führer. Death surrounds them, yet they break out the champagne and put on records for dancing. The hot jazz drowns out the whine of the ventilation system, because the party is hundreds of feet underground, deep beneath the Chancellery garden, where a bunker has been built to shield Hitler from the Russian bombs leveling Berlin.

Just the week before, Hitler still had hope, a grasping at straws, but hope nonetheless. Roosevelt had died, which Hitler took as a sign that the Reich would be saved. Just the day before, Goebbels had been reading to him from

The Life of Frederick the Great, the passage where Frederick contemplates suicide because the war seems to be lost. But then the empress of Russia dies and her heir ends the war, and so Frederick snatches victory from the jaws of defeat. "What Empress will die this time?" Hitler had asked dispiritedly, and as if in answer, the next day Roosevelt was dead.

For a brief time, everyone in the bunker celebrated and was joyful. Congratulations poured in from all sides. But Roosevelt's death in fact changes nothing, for Truman stays the course. Before long, the old despair settles over the occupants of the bunker.

Which is typical of the way Hitler and his circle perceive the world. Although they are unbelievers, who mock Christian "superstition," they themselves are superstitious to the nth degree, forever trying to read their fate in omens and signs and the stars.

Perhaps the "sign" to which Hitler attaches most meaning is his truly phenomenal luck in escaping assassination. Attempt after attempt is made on his life, but he always manages to survive by the skin of his teeth. A bomb is packed away in his plane, but it fails to explode. On another occasion, some obscure intuition or impulse prompts him to leave a Nazi anniversary celebration early, thus saving his life when a bomb goes off moments later, exploding right beneath the platform on which he was speaking.

The most miraculous escape of all is toward the end of the war, during the "generals' plot." A senior officer brings a briefcase loaded with explosives into the bunker as the Führer is holding a situation conference. The table on which the maps are spread is supported by a heavy slab of concrete. The officer puts down the briefcase and leaves. But just seconds before the explosion occurs, Hitler finds the briefcase in his way. Leaning over a map, he absent-mindedly puts the briefcase on the other side of the concrete slab, a gesture that saves his life. Though an eardrum is punctured and his pants are left in tatters, he is otherwise unhurt.

"Divine Providence saved me," he says afterward to his amazed entourage, sublimely unaware of the ridiculous, almost cartoonish figure he cuts. "I am meant to fulfill my mission."

Even as late as the day before, Hitler still had faith in this mission. He strode from room to room holding a disintegrating road map in his sweating, shaking hands as he explained to everyone in sight how General Wenck's Twentieth Army would soon come to the rescue. But now even he realizes that Wenck's army is a figment of his imagination, long since destroyed. Everything is over, and all that remains before he shoots himself in the mouth is . . . to get married. That will be his last act, he decides, to reward his faithful mistress, Eva Braun.

The young woman has been his mistress ever since Hitler's real obsession, his half-niece Geli Raubl, committed suicide. Pornographic drawings of Geli's private parts drawn (and signed) by Hitler must be bought up by the Nazi Party's treasurer from a blackmailer, along with "love letters" he wrote to her. The blackmailer, together with his landlady's son, who knew too much, will later end up dead, their bodies found in a wood outside Munich. Disgust, revulsion, and shame played a large part in Geli's suicide. Hitler could only get aroused through acts that revolted the girl—she would have to squat and pee on him—just as they also played a part in the suicide of Renate Müller, a movie star who had a short affair with Hitler, during which she would beat and kick him while he groveled in front of her, masturbating.

Complicating all this is Hitler's monorchism, the descent of only one testicle. The Russian autopsy of Hitler's charred corpse states that "the scrotal sac was burned but intact and the left testicle missing." The power of his hypnotic stare was in some measure a compensation, the eyes taking the place of the testicles. In many of Hitler's photographs, he stares out at the camera as if trying to subdue it, while his hands are crossed over his genitals in a protective gesture, or a hat or cap is held over his crotch.

Although the condition of monorchism does not make sexual intercourse physically impossible for Hitler, still, shame holds him back and perverts his relationship to his body. Throughout his life, he cannot bear being kissed. Even as a boy, when it is impossible to wake him, his mother will tell his sister, "Go kiss Adolf!" and he will jump out of bed in horror—a horror that only intensifies as he grows to manhood.

Early in his career, when he is invited to a New Year's party at the home of the Hanfstaengls, wealthy art publishers, a young woman kisses him unexpectedly under the mistletoe and Hitler flees, his fists clenched, his face drenched in sweat. No, for him sexuality is too dark an activity for carefree kisses. It is bound up with pain and humiliation.

The reason Hitler's affair with Eva Braun is different from his relationship to his half-niece is that it is not sexual, only romantic. "As a man I get nothing from him," Eva tells her sister Gretl, asking Hitler's doctor whether there is anything he can give the Führer to make him potent.

Yet her whole life revolves around "the Führer," which is what she calls him even in private. When he is away, she passes the time by playing sports, dancing to phonograph records, changing her clothes frequently, polishing her nails, reading movie magazines. She has no ideas apart from Hitler's, let alone an understanding of the evil he is perpetrating. She fits the Führer's definition of what a woman should be: "A childlike little thing, gentle and stupid." He would not want her to be more than she is; intelligent women make him uncomfortable.

Not that Hitler underestimates the value of women politically. No, it is precisely because he considers them an important political force that he declares he will never marry: he wants to be an object of their fantasy, and he senses that the picture of him with a wife would destroy this illusion.

It is a shrewd observation into the romance of power, for women will be very important in the development of the Nazi Party. Frau Bechstein, of the Bechstein piano family, is one of the first to welcome Hitler into her exclusive circle. She tells her husband that she would like to "adopt the young man." Hitler is already in his forties and she is a woman of sixty. He will lie with his head in her lap while she strokes his hair and reproaches him for his "excesses," though these very excesses are obviously what has drawn her to him. The outsider, the onetime inhabitant of Vienna's skid row, finds himself taking tea in the elegant garden of Mme. Sharer, heir to the St. Louis beer-brewing fortune. While peacocks stroll among the flower beds and swans float on the artificial lake, the rich and powerful husbands listen to Hitler's promises to destroy the Communist menace as the wives sit mesmerized by his hypnotic gaze.

Then there is Winifred Wagner, daughter-in-law of the great composer Richard Wagner. Born a British subject, she has become more German than the Germans, seeing in Wagner's operas the artistic expression of a great nationalistic political ideal. At Bayreuth, the city dedicated to Wagnerian opera, she receives Hitler with joy. And it is an important connection for Hitler, since the spirit behind Wagner's music is the spirit that inspires the Nazi movement.

The ancient German myths that Wagner sets to music will be revived by the Nazis, whose values are pagan, not Christian. It is not charity, love, and humility that are taught to the Nazi youth but hardness of heart, racial hatred, and physical strength. In Wagner's cycle of operas, a brother and sister commit incest; the child of this union is the hero-warrior Siegfried. The incest is an important aspect of the plot; it is a part of Wagner's glorification of the instinctual, the untamed, the primitive desires which have been repressed to create society. This is what draws Hitler to Wagner, because Hitler's appeal is also to the primitive, the deeply buried emotions in his audience. When he addresses the masses at the huge Nuremberg rallies, Hitler stirs up their hatred and brutality, their blood lust and thirst for military glory.

The world of Wagner's operas is the world of Hitler's imagination, the daydreams and nightmares of an insomniac. In the *Ring* cycle, the hero Siegfried sets out to win the gold ring that will enable him to rule the world. But this ring, forged through the renunciation of love, is cursed, and inevitably brings death to its possessor and universal destruction. The music from Wagner's "Immolation scene," when the world is consumed in "purifying" flames, is the music Hitler orders played across the nation as Berlin, as all of Germany, is bombed into submission. It is an extreme example, characteristic of Hitler, of life made to imitate art even at the cost of life's annihilation.

The charade to be played out in the bunker, the wedding-funeral of Hitler and Eva Braun, would come straight out of Wagner's *Tristan and Isolde,* in which the "Liebestod," the love-death music, celebrates the Wagnerian motif of love being consummated in death. In welcoming Hitler to Bayreuth, where he becomes known to the Wagner grandchildren as "the uncle with the gun in his pocket," Winifred Wagner is welcoming a kindred soul. Her admiration for him is bound up with her admiration for the myth of Germany as Wagner staged it and set it to music in the titanic spectacle of his operas. After the war, when most Germans will strive to disassociate themselves from the Nazi horrors and will profess that they had nothing to do with Hitler, Winifred Wagner, unrepentant—more, still proud of being an early member of the Party—will say that the Allies found only *one* Nazi when they conquered Germany: an old British woman named Winifred.

But it is not only prominent women like Mme. Wagner or the wives of financiers and socialites who take up Hitler. Working women and mothers, schoolgirls and older women swarm around the Führer, fainting during his speeches, throwing themselves in front of his car, even asking for his bathwater when he is sentenced to a year in the Landsberg prison for the putsch of 1923. The prison becomes a kind of shrine to Hitler, his cell overflowing with boxes of chocolates and sweets, groups of women throwing flowers up at his windows. His mistake of trying to overthrow the state by force means a year in jail, but it also enhances his romantic appeal. In the end it will be this legend, the fiery speeches, the pose, the image that will win the day for him. He emerges from jail a hero.

Of all his women followers, Hitler is particularly fond of the elderly "respectable" women who moan and get misty-eyed at his rallies. He makes sure the first few rows are reserved for them, the "varicose-vein brigade," as they are known among his bodyguards.

In fact, so important is this bond between Hitler and

his female followers that when the tide of war turns and Hitler orders that every factory and business not absolutely necessary for the war effort or survival be shut down, the one exception he makes is the beauty parlors. "I will not do anything to dampen the enthusiasm of our women," he insists, a concession to female vanity which is insulting and patronizing, of course, and in keeping with his view of women's shallow nature.

And so it is that, up until these last hours in the bunker, he has steadfastly proclaimed his intention never to take a wife: for the Savior of Germany it would not be fitting. Eva must always be kept out of sight whenever important visitors are around. In fact, the German people will only find out about her after the war. But now that the end is near, she insists on leaving Hitler's Alpine retreat to die with him in Berlin. And Hitler, pleased by her loyalty, has decided to pair their suicide with their nuptials.

The small group in the bunker will witness the solemn ceremony. Goebbels is, after the Führer, the highest in rank present. He has decided to kill himself once Hitler is dead. He knows there is no future for him and that there is nowhere he can flee, since he is almost as well known as the leader. He has brought his wife and their six young children to die with him in the bunker. As the wedding preparations go forward, the older girl watches the bride get ready, putting on the makeup that her groom-to-be disapproves of: "French lipstick—I would hate to tell you ladies what it is made of," Hitler often says. "Waste water!" It is a telling comment, in view of his sexual preferences. The younger children scamper nearby playing hide-and-seek, unaware that lethal injections will soon put an end to all their games.

Then there are Hitler's secretaries, to each of whom the bride will give a keepsake of the day. First there is

Christa Daranowsky, a heavy-hipped, dark-haired woman, formerly an employee of Elizabeth Arden, now devoted to the Führer. He has even chosen a husband for her from among his officers, which is not unusual for those who work for Hitler, given his mania for matchmaking. There is also the youngest secretary, Traudl Junge, married at his "suggestion" to his valet. The granddaughter of a German general, she is the one most oppressed by the atmosphere of defeat hanging over Hitler in the last months; her illusions about Nazism gradually crumble as she works for Hitler.

Finally there is Christa Schroeder, who never liked Eva but who helps adorn the bride. She must bite her lips to keep back the tears, a rare display of emotion for her. The always efficient Shroeder will take down Hitler's last testament, a rambling, self-pitying document. In it he blames the Jews for having started the war. "But though they have caused this disaster," he tells the world, "I will go laughing into the grave, having killed so many millions of them." Schroeder has worked for the Führer since the beginning and has heard his monologues a thousand times. Yet for her he is still the "great man," and she treats his every utterance as if it must be preserved for all time.

One task that must be fulfilled before the wedding begins is to take care of a matter of "justice." Eva's sister Gretl is married to an SS general, Hermann Fegelein. That morning he slipped out of the Führer bunker to climb the endless flights of steps toward the light. As the heavy metal gate clanged shut behind him he sighed with relief, squinting at the light of day for the first time in a week. Then he made a dash for it, sprinting through the nearby streets and past the Tiergarten, the abandoned zoo, where the starving inhabitants of Berlin have killed and eaten the beasts. With great difficulty he crossed the city to his apartment in Charlottenburg.

Not only did he have to be wary of bombs and falling buildings, but military patrols were everywhere. Even boys of twelve and thirteen have been recruited for this last desperate battle to save Berlin, as Fegelein well knows, having stood next to Hitler as the Führer pinned medals on the chests of these children, stroking their downy cheeks with his palsied hands and staring into their eyes with his demonic gaze.

Children though they are, if they had caught Fegelein in the act of deserting they would have shot him on the spot, SS general or no; those are the Führer's orders. So Fegelein kept a lookout for the German patrols as well as for the Russian soldiers who have encircled the city, getting closer to the bunker day by day. He was on his way to meet a beautiful countess, the wife of a Hungarian diplomat, with whom he planned to flee the city. It would have been a shame to die with a beauty like the countess waiting for him.

But Hitler, even with his world going to pieces around him, notices Fegelein's absence. He asks Eva about it, but she has no idea where her sister's husband has gone. Hitler sends an adjutant to Gretl Braun to find out. But Gretl, pregnant with her first child and suffering from intense morning sickness, thought that her husband was with the Führer.

"Find him! Arrest him!" Hitler orders when the adjutant returns with this news, and within the hour the unlucky Fegelein is brought back to the bunker surrounded by guards.

"Coward!" Hitler shouts, ripping the epaulettes and medals off Fegelein's uniform. "Traitor! What can you say for yourself?"

But Fegelein, like all high-ranking members of the army or gestapo, has seen the Führer in his insane rages.

Hitler will throw himself down and gnaw on the carpet as he pounds his fists against the floor, or, worse, he will quickly dismiss the object of his displeasure, who will suddenly find him- or herself on the steps of the Chancellery, hustled into a car, and on the way to a concentration camp. There is nothing better than silence at such a moment, Fegelein knows. And that's just the tack he takes, lowering his eyes and throwing back his broad shoulders. Fegelein, tall, good-looking, with the "Aryan" features of blond hair and blue eyes, is the picture of contrition. He stands humbly before his leader.

"Lock him in one of the rooms!" Hitler orders his bodyguards, to everyone's surprise. Being the husband of Eva's sister has saved him, it is whispered, although Eva has not said a word in his defense. From long habit she has learned to submit to the Führer's will.

Later in the day, however, Fegelein's treachery will be seen in a different light. An intelligence officer whose job it is to monitor foreign broadcasts picks up a shocking piece of news. The head of the gestapo, Heinrich Himmler, Fegelein's chief, has offered to surrender to the Allies in the West. It is inconceivable: Himmler, "the loyal Heinrich," as Hitler always calls him, has deserted. When the dispatch is read out loud, the men and women in the bunker shriek with rage and fear like lunatics. And Hitler is worst of all. His face is reddish purple, his body trembles, his head shakes uncontrollably, and his voice is even more terrifying in the hoarse whisper it has become: "Shoot them all! Kill every one of them!"

Who must be shot? Who does he mean? Himmler? Himmler's officers? The British and American prisoners of war? The Russians encircling Berlin? It almost doesn't matter, for Hitler's every other word now is "kill." Earlier, Hitler muttered that the officers of the German air force, all of them without exception, should be shot for having allowed things to come to this pass.

For a moment Hitler stands stock-still, holding on to a chair as if he were about to collapse. Then he turns to Hanna Reitsch, a daredevil pilot who has just arrived. Through a sky filled with dogfights, she has flown into Berlin, skillfully maneuvering her plane and flying low over trees and buildings. Russian searchlights had picked up her plane and it was strafed with flak, but still, somehow, she had managed to bring it out of a nosedive and land on the broad avenue near the Brandenburg Gate.

By the light of burning buildings she has made her way to the bunker, hoping to die with her Führer. But several surprises await her. Her first shock is finding her hero so aged and palsied. His head wobbles; he drags one leg as he walks; he can barely hold a magnifying glass steady as he tries to read dispatches. Her second shock is to meet Eva Braun, to find that Hitler has a mistress, a girl half his age who flits around the bunker in fashionable clothes. Hanna's final shock is to learn that though she has flown all the way to Berlin through incredible danger to die with her Führer, he will not allow her to end her life after all. No, instead Hitler orders her to return.

"Hanna! You must fly out immediately!" he commands her, gently taking her hands in his and looking into her eyes. "A traitor must never succeed me as Führer! You must make sure that Himmler is stripped of his offices! He must die!"

Weeping quietly, Hanna bows her head and submits to Hitler's wishes.

Hitler writes out some orders for her, and Eva Braun entrusts her with a farewell letter she has written her sister Gretl, a letter that will never arrive. Later Hanna cannot resist reading it, and then tears it to bits, scandalized at its puerility, she will say. She is jealous, too, because *she* is not the woman in Hitler's life.

Taking her leave, Hanna salutes her Führer for the last time and makes her way to her plane, in which she accomplishes a second miracle: with great skill and bravery, she manages to fly out of the war-torn city. But when she arrives at her destination she finds that a new wave of American bombings has taken place. Among the other buildings destroyed in Munich, the Party headquarters, the Brown House, has been leveled, killing everyone inside. The daredevil pilot has succeeded in delivering the Führer's orders—but she has brought them to men who are dead.

III. IN THE BUNKER: A COURT MARTIAL AND A PAIR OF GLOVES

My idea of justice—cut off a man's head or let him go free!
—Adolf Hitler

Having bid farewell to Hanna Reitsch, Hitler now turns to Fegelein. He has been locked up since morning, forgotten by all except his Hungarian countess, who will never make it to the border without him, and by the SS bodyguards who have been going through his possessions. Almost comically, it has been discovered that he has stolen some of Eva Braun's jewelry; bracelets and earrings the Führer gave her have been tucked away, along with a portrait of Hitler set in diamonds, a curiously romantic touch. A love letter from the countess has also been found, revealing Fegelein's plan to desert his pregnant wife.

Fegelein the opportunist is a fitting symbol of the nation: within a week of Hitler's suicide, the Nazi movement will be no more. No other major political movement in history has ever disappeared so quickly after its founder's death. It has been a mirage, a nightmare, and at its core have been emptiness, nihilism, the longing for death and destruction. In a sense, *Fegelein* is Hitler—just without the genius.

During the Reich, Hitler has ranted and raved about his great love for the German people. But it is all theater, all pretense; they are only a tool for his glory. And now in the bunker his mask falls away. For he has decided that if he must die, then the German nation should perish as well. "It has proved itself unworthy of me," he says, ordering Speer, his minister of armaments, to destroy every factory, every bridge, every power plant in Germany. "It is not necessary to worry about what the German people will need for elemental survival. On the contrary, it is best for us to destroy even these things. For the nation has proved to be the weaker, and the future belongs to the stronger Russian nation. In any case, only those who are inferior will remain after this struggle, for the good have already been killed." His orders are never carried out. Speer has no qualms working hundreds of thousands of Poles, Russians, and Jews to death in his armaments factories, but he is unable to cause the death of so many of his countrymen.

As it is, though, even without these desperate measures many will die during the Führer's last days in the bunker. His murderous impulses have been aroused, and even though he is hundreds of feet underground in a besieged city, just the sound of his hoarse voice over the static of the shaky communication system is enough. His word is still law.

Fegelein will be one of these last-minute victims. At first Hitler had been willing to pardon him. After all, he is an SS general and Hitler is partial to the SS—his "Society of Jesus," he calls them, comparing them to Loyola's fervent Jesuits. But the news about Himmler has changed all that. Now that their chief has proved himself a traitor, it casts doubt on all of them, especially Fegelein, Himmler's liaison at the Führer's headquarters during the last year. Taking place at the same time as Himmler's betrayal, what did Fegelein's desertion that morning mean? Surely his desertion was not just a moment's cowardice, Hitler reasons, but part of a larger plot.

The unlucky SS general is brought before Hitler, and the Führer stares at him with contempt. "Take off his belt!" he shouts. The SS motto, "Our loyalty is our honor," is inscribed on the buckle.

A bizarre court martial now begins, the deserter starting to defend himself with a pathetic reference to his rank: "As a general of the SS, may I say—" But Hitler interrupts him, spewing insults and scorn. He concludes with the question that will seal Fegelein's fate: "And how did the general conduct himself during that most difficult of all missions?"

It is a roundabout way of asking Fegelein about his part in the mass murders of civilians during the invasion of Poland and Russia, the crime that, as Hitler knows, binds together the Nazi brotherhood of the damned. It is the surest sign of loyalty. The accused tries to stammer out an answer, but Hitler sneers. He has heard about Fegelein's squeamishness, a failing he has overlooked for the sake of Eva's sister but one which is inexcusable in an SS man. For the SS were created to fulfill a darker mission than mere conquest. First came the blitzkrieg, the lightning war without warning fought by the regular troops; then came the Einsatzgruppen, the brutal death squads that cast a shadow over the defeated peoples.

In the beginning, in Poland, even the military complains to the Führer about the atrocities. The SS show no mercy to young or old; even pregnant women and children are tortured and murdered. But Hitler brushes aside the military's objections. Since his earliest days his plan has been to level Moscow, Hitler confides to his secretaries over coffee with *schlag*. "Yes, to wipe it from the face of the earth so that no one will guess that a city existed there. To bomb Leningrad into a lake, destroy its dams and canals, flood the city so that German tourists can go boating there. The vast expanses across Russia, Poland, and the East will be German colonies. The most intelligent part of the population will be put to death. The rest will be used for slave labor, not taught how to read, or maybe just enough to read the signs to keep off the roads as the Germans drive through the conquered territory."

By the time the German army passes through the Ukraine on its way to Moscow, the mass graves and the portable gas vans are a familiar sight. Fegelein, however, will never acquire the stomach for such sights. He lacks the qualities necessary to succeed in the "sacred mission." And Fegelein is not alone in his squeamishness, for some of the tough brawlers of the SS end up suffering what can be called nervous breakdowns after massacring thousands of victims; they are haunted by the sounds and smells and sights and cannot go on.

But if the sensitive are not to be entrusted with this mission, neither are the sadists who enjoy killing and rape; they are equally unfit in Hitler's eyes, because the slaughter only whets their appetite for more. He wants his men to be strong beasts of prey, but he also wants restraint. Control. He sees the slaughter as *work,* as their *duty,* which they must be hardened to perform. "Only the strong will survive, and so the German people must be strong." The nation needs *lebensraum,* room in which to expand, and that will naturally be the vast expanses of Russia. Such is Hitler's line, endlessly repeated to his high command and down to the rawest recruit.

But General Fegelein is not made from such "idealistic" stuff; the piles of entwined corpses sicken him. Accompanying his chief, Himmler, to the Ukraine, Fegelein arrives at a clearing in the woods where ditches are filled with bodies frozen in their death agonies. He covers his eyes with his hands to keep from fainting, a lapse that at first goes unnoticed because Himmler is preoccupied with a blue-eyed blond boy standing with the Jews lined up for execution.

"Do you have one non-Jewish parent?" Himmler asks him, struck by his "Aryan" characteristics.

The youth shakes his head.

"What about your grandparents? Were they *all* Jewish?"

"Yes," the young man answers bravely, refusing the invitation to live a lie.

"Then there is nothing I can do for you!" Himmler shouts, giving a signal for the massacre to continue. Shots ring out, and together with the rest of the victims, the youth falls backward into the ditch he has just dug—at the sight of which Fegelein starts to vomit. In shame the general rushes to his tent, where he finds consolation in pills and liquor, the pills courtesy of Dr. Morell.

A specialist in venereal diseases, Morell was originally asked to treat the Führer for his uncontrollable flatulence. Morell prescribes unorthodox gas pills made from belladonna, strychnine, and atropine. Hitler will take these pills in great quantity right up until the end, ignoring the symptoms of strychnine poisoning that begin to develop, sensitivity to light, unbearable stomach cramps, and blinding headaches, his hoarse throat and the strange reddish tinge of his skin.

Soon Morell also has Hitler addicted to all kinds of stimulants, by injection, which he administers before the great speeches and rallies. There is sympatol to quicken Hitler's heart and there are injections of Vitamultin, the obese doctor's own concoction of pervitin and caffeine. And there is prostacrinum, an extract of seminal vesicles and prostate to prevent depression—all these are given to Hitler, along with whatever else enters Morell's head to try.

But the inventive doctor has remedies for small occasions as well as great ones, and the pills soon make Fegelein forget his great shortcoming, that is, his lack of the brutal coldness that Hitler touts as a sign of the superior man. To tell the truth, though, Hitler himself is far from being this kind of idealized murderer. Although the Führer preaches ruthlessness in the struggle for survival— "I know only one thing," he says, "to strike, strike, and strike again!"—Hitler cannot face the human consequences of his own philosophy.

During the years he is in power, Hitler will never visit a concentration camp. He cannot even bear to hear his atrocities described in such a way that puts a human face on them. A young woman invited to dinner decides to take her life in her hands and reproach Hitler for what is going on. Perhaps she counts on the fact that her father is his favorite photographer. Or perhaps she remembers an early incident, years before, when Hitler was just building up the Nazi Party. He would visit her father's house, and on one occasion took an "interest" in her, even though she was then barely in her teens. He had come close and held out his hands to her when they were alone, but she had rebuffed his advance.

"Please, Herr Hitler," she had said, "it is not possible for me." It is an incident about which her father fearfully warned her to remain silent, since even then, Hitler was a powerful man.

Now, attending a dinner party with her husband, Baldur von Shirach, the head of the Hitler Youth, she interrupts the conversation to relate with horror and pity what she has seen and heard on a recent trip to Amsterdam: the heartrending cries of Jewish women being rounded up for slaughter, the young Jewish girls being dragged into gestapo cars.

It is brave; it is an astonishing act. The others at the table sit frozen with embarrassment as she appeals to their humanity. And Hitler becomes furious. For lesser crimes than hers, people have been sent to concentration camps; but the Führer merely sends her away, banishing her from his presence forever, though not to the camps. For the rest of the evening, it seems as if he will change his mind about her any minute, that she stands on the edge of a precipice. He clasps his hands until the knuckles are white and mutters to himself. She has unnerved him by bringing the reality of the suffering too close.

Similarly, once German casualties begin to mount, Hitler can never bring himself to visit his wounded soldiers. He cannot stand the sight of them and keeps clear of the hospitals, not to mention the German cities that have been reduced to rubble by Allied bombers. Hitler keeps the shades of his train windows down if he has to pass through those cities; nothing could be more dreadful in his eyes. When Goebbels, who makes regular tours to boost morale, meets citizens wandering among their ruined homes, they ask him, "Where is our Führer?" only to be given posters with photos of him in knight's armor or in a storm trooper's uniform over the ironic slogan "Hitler is victory!"

This is also true on a personal level. When secretary Traudl Junge's husband is killed at the front, Hitler tries to tell her and fails. He is overwhelmed. As it happens, General Fegelein is on hand, and in this respect, at least, the handsome SS man is stronger than his leader; he consoles the young woman, the prettiest of the secretaries, comforting her so well that he exceeds his orders.

Brash, confident, uncaring, Fegelein loves horses, brawling, swaggering, sensation, style, and women—and women love him. Even now, as he faces death, Traudl Junge watches him from the doorway; it is hard for her to hide how much she cares about his fate.

"A worthless lout!" Hitler suddenly breaks off the proceedings, having heard enough. The verdict is pronounced: "Take him up to the garden and shoot him!" Instantly, Fegelein is dragged from the Führer's presence.

"How has such a man risen to the rank of general?" Hitler wants to know, pursuing this irrelevance as if Russian troops were not coming closer to the bunker at every moment. Which is characteristic of the way the Führer has conducted the war all along: he becomes obsessed with trivialities, wasting hours on details that could be left to subordinates, poring over statistics and charts he uses to support decisions he has already made.

If the facts do not fit his theories, so much the worse for the facts. At a meeting of the general staff in 1942, for example, he comes close to striking a general who reads a report warning of the vast reserves of the Russian army; the general's orderly must pull his chief back as Hitler fumes, shaking his fist in the man's face. "Stop reading that twaddle!" he shouts. "And have the man who wrote it locked up in an insane asylum!" Then he starts reeling off statistics about the German war machine, revealing a phenomenal memory that retains the most minute details— but to what purpose? He might as well be reciting baseball trivia for all it matters.

He indulges in the same kind of futile preoccupation

now, brooding about Fegelein as the gestapo liaison is dragged up to the garden. "How can it be that such a coward and weakling won the Cross of the Knight?" the Führer demands, glaring at Fegelein's erstwhile colleagues as if they too have betrayed him.

"Maybe for his service in the Castles, *mein Führer,*" one of the adjutants suggests; a clever suggestion, for the "Castles," the Nazi military institutes, are a sure road to promotion in the Third Reich. They are chosen as the training ground for a handpicked few, and completion of the curriculum, personally drawn up by Hitler, permits the graduate to join the Nazi elite.

At this mention of the Castles Hitler pauses, pacified for the moment, for they are an embodiment of everything he believes in. Shrouded in the romance of the past, reviving ancient knightly rituals and codes, the Castles are designed to inspire their students with absolute loyalty. "If Fegelein is a product of this knightly order," Hitler remarks, beginning one of his endless monologues, "then he is the exception that proves the rule. For in such sublime settings, the candidates learn to die for . . ." Hitler rambles on, distracted.

No one mentions how strange it is to think of the illiterate Fegelein's graduating from any educational institution, no less Germany's new "West Point." Just eight years earlier, in the 1930s, the future SS general could barely scrawl love notes to the frauleins who found their way into his bed over the stables at the Daglfing Racetrack, where he worked with the horses and took bets on the side.

But then, the military academy is not what it was: an aristocratic and formidable institution dedicated to the science of warfare. In the Third Reich that kind of institute is no more, and perhaps Fegelein's background is just what it should be. For Hitler despises the generals of the old school, and with good reason, too, since all of those monocled and steel-helmeted gentlemen have tried to discourage him at each step along the way—Czechoslovakia, Poland, Norway, France, Russia—warning him that he was leading the country to disaster. They formed a Greek chorus, advising him to pull back, to moderate his demands, to wait, to show caution and restraint—not to take the big gamble.

But he, the "little Austrian corporal" as they mockingly called him among themselves because of his rank in World War I and the allusion to Napoleon; he, the "hysterical rabble rouser" they thought they would use for their own ends; he, the amateur, the outsider with no formal military training but with an instinct for the game, proved that he was right. He had won by breaking all the rules while they, the professional gentlemen, had been proved wrong.

After the war, Hitler's armaments minister Speer will write that these early victories set the stage for the Nazi downfall. They intoxicated both the nation and its leader, making him deaf to reason and convincing him of his infallibility. When the generals try to offer their perspective during the Russian campaign they are scorned. "Nazi ardor is what is needed now," he tells them, "not professionalism."

On this basis, during the Russian campaign Hitler will finally dismiss his chief of operations. He himself will assume complete control over the army. Thus he removes the last reasonable check on his passions and manias. "Who better to train the army in the Nazi spirit than I?" he asks. "More important than tactics is the will to victory—victory or death!"

And so it is for this purpose, to inspire the new generation of commanders with the Nazi spirit, that Hitler establishes the Castles, the four schools in which he re-creates the atmosphere of the fourteenth-century Teutonic knights. The Castles are a historical fantasy brought to life, with a Nazi twist. The leading principle is absolute obedi-ence to the Master of the Order—the Führer. And the goal is twofold: the expansion of German culture eastward and the enslavement of the Poles and Russians.

To help populate this vast territory which Hitler is bent on conquering, the candidates are invited to take part in the activities of another SS organization, the Lebensborn, the "Spring of Life." Here young women who have pure "Aryan" characteristics—blue eyes, blond hair, Nordic features, a measurement of the skull that fits Nazi standards—volunteer to mate with storm troopers to improve the racial stock; the children, who are to be wards of the state, will eventually, Hitler hopes, breed out the "dark Germans" (such as himself) in favor of a "more pure" national type. The Lebensborn also arranges for the kidnapping of thousands of children from the conquered countries who display the desired characteristics. A fact kept from the general population is that Hitler does not consider the entire German nation Aryan, or pure Aryan; just as the nation is unaware that the retarded and insane are being put to death in the name of the Führer's attempt to breed a "Master Race." All that is announced is that the Lebensborn officials encourage Aryans to couple; and the youths in the Castles are viewed as prime candidates. They are expected to perform sexual relations for "the sake of duty," regardless of romantic feelings or lack of in-terest in marriage.

But apart from this duty, the young men in the Castles must remain chaste, their minds free from lust, concen-trated on studies such as "race science," the Nazis' quack racial theories, and the pseudoscience of phrenology, an interpretation of the size of the skull and its bumps and shape, supposed to reveal character and intelligence. Physically, they prepare for war by mountain climbing and parachute jumping; spiritually, by studying the words of the Führer. The final training takes place in Marienburg, in the same gloomy, thick-walled castle that had been a fortress of the Teutonic knights five centuries before.

It is not only the military institutes that Hitler makes over in his own image but *all* the schools in the Reich. Psychology is denounced as a Jewish invention. Indeed, all branches of study now must be approved from the Nazi point of view if they are to be taught. In physics, Einstein is dismissed as a subhuman taking part in a Jewish conspiracy to corrupt science in its pure, Nordic form. In chemistry, in engineering, in field after field, the Germans fall behind as they insist on a Nazi version of reality.

"Nazi enthusiasm is more important than truth"—that is the standard Hitler sets. Even "Nazi" art is separated from the "degenerate" sort: Picasso and van Gogh are mocked while trivial Nazi artists are extolled. The new generation is won over with torchlit parades, songs, gymnastics, hate sessions (for the Slav and Jew), love sessions (for the Master Race), the Hitler Youth, the German Maidens Union, and the Strength-Through-Joy Organization where the cities' youth throw off their shackles in pagan communion with nature (the result of which is an unprecedented rise in teenage pregnancy, giving rise to the standing joke: "I lost my strength through joy"). Everyone, from kindergarten children to distinguished professors, must daily repeat the pledge with fervor: "I swear to devote all my strength to the savior of our country, Adolf Hitler. I am willing to give up my life for him, so help me God."

So the Führer becomes all-knowing, directing the education and consciousness of an entire nation. But what does he himself actually know? From his earliest youth, he has been incapable of sustained, disciplined intellectual work. He barely manages to complete high school and is the most mediocre of students. Showing some skill in drawing, he wants to be an artist or architect, but his dreams are opposed by his father, a rigid Austrian customs official. His mother dotes on the boy, though, and after her husband's death lets him go off to Vienna to make his way.

Vienna, Hitler's five years there, will form him. Rejected both for art and architecture by the Viennese Academy, the young man slowly sinks into poverty and the life of a vagabond. Free of the usual vices—he does not drink or smoke and is shy with women—he devours the newspapers and becomes obsessed with politics. He lives at a men's shelter, where he subsists on bread and soup, sometimes earning a pittance by shoveling snow or selling the nondescript watercolors and drawings he produces.

When he gets into arguing politics with his fellow down-and-outers he will sometimes go into a frenzy, shouting and waving his arms about so that they are either astonished or provoked to laughter at this outlandish, hysterical fellow. And indeed he makes a strange picture, sitting on the edge of his bed in his lice-ridden clothes, spewing hatred, threats, and world-prophecies. It is unimaginable that such a man, on the brink of lunacy, will one day be chancellor of Germany.

Sometimes he will spend days reading whatever happens to be available in the public library; there is no rhyme or reason in his selection: works on ancient Greece, primitive religion, hypnotism, astrology, German history, yoga, the latest anti-Semitic pamphlets, water-divining, and philosophy, especially Nietzsche, whose words he twists to his own vision. Even this haphazard study can make very little difference in the young Hitler's development; what he reads, like the military statistics he learns, is always put to the same use: to confirm what he already believes.

Sometimes his bouts of reading and energetic argument give way, very suddenly, to despondency and sloth. At these times, Hitler, together with whatever vagabond he can bend to his will, devises petty stratagems to survive: he may roast a painting he has done and manage to sell it as an antique, say, but all it means is a week or so of good dining or a new pair of shoes.

He is ignorant, then, yet professors, playwrights, and philosophers hail him as the savior they have been waiting for. Heidegger will praise him for having taken "unconditional responsibility for the fate of the German people," and the great philosopher's endorsement will boost the regime's prestige abroad. Even the distinguished generals of the German general staff knuckle under to him, however reluctantly. Hitler is applauded as the conqueror of Europe, a Zeitgeist, a genius and world-spirit. You can't argue with success—unless you have a conscience and the heart to consider at what price that success has been purchased. But the Germans are too shaken by what they have been through, and they welcome a savior. World War I has brought them poverty, despair, a rate of inflation so fantastically high that when a thief overturns a basket filled with money in the street, he is after the basket, not the money.

Hitler knows how to play on their despair and anger. Ultimately, knowledge is not what has given Hitler his success; his instincts have. He is no stranger to hatred and envy and uses these to build a rapport with the crowd and its primitive emotions. He is a genius in using the rhythms of his speeches, the gestures of his hands, the slow buildup to unrestrained fury which is picked up and echoed by the crowd. It is right to speak of Hitler's "calling," because there is a kind of dark artistry in it—as well as something akin to sexual release, the fulfillment he can never get with women.

As a young man, the first time Hitler sees a movie with an orator in it—Kellerman's *The Tunnel,* in which an agitator stirs up a crowd—he becomes almost crazy with excitement, wandering around in a daze for hours afterward. "The power of the spoken word was revealed to me," he writes. And indeed it is like a revelation to the would-be dictator, whose discovery of his own genius as a speaker will be a second revelation, of equal importance.

Long before he gives his first public speech, from his earliest youth his need to talk, explain, theorize, expound is almost like a physical pressure. During adolescence this will make Hitler friendless, until he meets August Kubizek, a classmate willing to listen for hours at a time who becomes his one companion. Without knowing it, Hitler is preparing for his future even then, putting gesture, emotion, and phrase together in long practice sessions with his friend.

His first "real" experience at oratory comes with the end of World War I. And though a fateful moment, it comes almost by chance. The war changes Hitler's life. He is transformed from a drifting vagabond into a soldier, and this new role of his gives him a reason to exist—the Fatherland. Far from complaining about the trenches, he embraces life in the army. The stench, the poor food, the danger and discomfort, nothing discourages him. He becomes a front-line runner in the German army, forsaking his native Austria, since he despises its "mongrel" mix of nationalities. Germany is the "homeland."

It's easy to see why the other men dislike him: he never talks about women, never receives packages from home (by this time, his mother has died of cancer, cared for by a Jewish doctor). He never longs for the end of the war, never even drinks or smokes. When provisions are so scarce that the men are reduced to eating dogs and cats, Hitler gets into a fistfight with a fellow soldier who says that the war is lost. "Only cowards and Jews talk that way!" Hitler shouts, though the battalion adjutant, Hugo Gutmann, is a Jew. Courting death, he volunteers for the most dangerous missions with a fanatic joy.

Germany's surrender finds him in a military hospital, suffering temporary blindness as a result of a mustard gas attack. He begins to rave incoherently and is transferred to a psychiatric ward, where his persistent blindness is now diagnosed as hysterical. During these long weeks of blindness and defeat and madness, he experiences a vision of almost mystical intensity. It is a vision of himself as Germany's savior and of the Jews as a kind of fatal bacillus that infects and destroys the healthy nations.

Finally he, among many, is declared "cured" and released from the hospital. The soldiers are released in droves, fit or unfit, cured or still suffering; the war has been lost and the authorities don't much care about these men.

His chest covered with medals his fanaticism has won him, Hitler reports for duty in a replacement brigade. All around him in the defeated army he finds disillusionment, disorder, unwillingness to obey orders. Officers are even laughed at when they call the soldiers to fall in. The harsh conditions of the peace and the crushing indemnity owed the Allies help destabilize the country. Radical Soviet groups struggle to take over the state, setting up a short-lived communist republic in Munich and seizing key buildings in Berlin. Equally radical right-wing forces form the Freikorps, and in the brutal fighting that follows, the Soviets are defeated. The Republic is established in Weimar because Berlin is still too dangerous.

From its birth, the Republic is undermined by the army, whose officers want an authoritarian regime. And one day, by chance, an officer happens to hear Hitler haranguing one of his fellow soldiers. *This man is perfect!* the officer thinks, immediately assigning him to the army's political indoctrination program, the army being intent on molding its soldiers into a political weapon.

Hitler attends an obligatory series of lectures given by ultranationalist, ultra-right-wing speakers. But Hitler could be the one lecturing *them,* as is soon apparent when he begins to address the men. His mixture of threat, promise, apology for the loss of the war is just what the dispirited soldiers want to hear. "The army only lost the war because of liberals back home agitating for peace" is the line he takes. "Germany would have been victorious if it had not been stabbed in the back by the Jews and liberals." Meanwhile, he is perfecting the art that will bring him to the leadership of Germany: as a speaker, he is unrivaled.

Sent by the army to investigate a small workers' party, which he will eventually turn into the Nazi Party, Hitler rises to answer some of the points made by the speaker and ends up making a speech himself. He talks long and fervently, causing the dozen or so men gathered for the meeting to become wild with excitement. Drexler, the party's founder, a locksmith, presses a pamphlet into Hitler's hands and urges him to join. Though the young soldier has little interest in becoming a member of anyone else's party, he is flattered by the attention and within a few meetings has taken control of the party's agenda. Word gets out about this amazing new speaker and attendance at the meetings quickly doubles, triples, quadruples. Hitler is on his way.

The speeches, some as long as three or four hours, are all carefully planned: Hitler himself seems to be carried away in a sea of emotion, but every moment is rehearsed down to the last detail. Before a major speech, he will delay for days, working on a phrase, thinking about a gesture, practicing before a mirror. His secretary writes out his notes on a special oversized typewriter so that he does not have to use the glasses he needs, which would not fit the image of the warrior-leader he is so eager to project. Trying different voices, he will ask his valet, Linge, "Do I sound enough like the Führer?" as if "the Führer" is a role he must assume.

The audiences keep getting larger, the party organization has become formidable, and by 1923 Hitler feels that he is ready for a grab at power. The coup is to take place in Munich, and from here Hitler hopes to proceed with a "march on Berlin," thus ending the Republic. Commissar von Kahr, one of a triumvirate controlling Munich, has called for a patriotic demonstration in a beer hall on the night of November 8, 1923. Kahr himself is addressing the crowd when suddenly Hitler and his storm troopers break in, blocking the exits and hustling the speakers off the platform. The crowd is in an uproar. Hitler fires shots into the air, demanding silence as he announces that the national revolution has begun.

He is pale, pasty-faced, wild-eyed, with a stray lock of hair flattened down against his brow, a strange figure dressed in an ill-fitting, absurd-looking formal morning coat.

At first people look at him with astonishment and scorn. Who is this laughable character that proclaims himself Germany's savior? But as he speaks he gradually captures the crowd. He knows their desires better than they themselves do. He is filled with enthusiasm and fanatical passion. And by the end of his talk he has worked his magic—the thundering *"Sieg Heils,"* the roars of approval, the hysteria of the crowd uniting as one being.

As it turns out, the coup is premature. After leaving the beer hall, Hitler marches toward the Hall of Heroes with his followers who include General Ludendorff, a hero of World War I who like Hitler despises the democratic Republic, and there is a confrontation with the state police. When a few shots are fired, Hitler falls to the ground instinctively, his only injury a dislocated shoulder from the fall. It is like a comic opera revolution, and yet the putsch actually ends up enhancing the Führer's reputation, as rumor and exaggeration make Hitler a hero.

During his trial for sedition, Hitler once again turns his oratory to effect, speaking for two and three hours at a stretch in a performance that will bring him national recognition. He is sentenced to a year in prison, where he will write *Mein Kampf* (*"My Struggle"*), his political autobiography. It is a turgid and rambling book, filled with his ideas on every subject from art to syphilis—*"the* most important question facing the nation," he writes, dwelling morbidly on this, another one of his lifelong sexual obsessions.

Released from prison, where the warden and jailers weep upon bidding him farewell, he is at first banned from public speaking in Germany. But there are too many powerful forces impressed by him—the industrialists, the army, the displaced working people whose economic suffering he has promised to relieve—for the ban to remain in effect long.

There are to be many more speeches, only as time goes on, spectacle and grandeur will be added. There will be music and a sea of flags and endless rows of goose-stepping troops to set Hitler off to his greatest advantage. And a flag of blood will commemorate the martyrs, because the Führer understands, of course, the need for martyrs. In fact, one of the most stirring moments at the Nazi rallies is the singing of the "Horst Wessel" anthem, a song Hitler has commissioned to honor a storm trooper killed "fighting the communists."

Never mind that in reality Horst Wessel was a pimp whose prostitute got tired of supporting him. The girl asks her landlady to help kick him out, and when the older woman calls in some street toughs, Wessel gets into a fight and is killed. From such stuff are Nazi martyrs made.

Cynically, Hitler orders the funeral to be staged as a major demonstration, with Nazi flags and tributes to the fallen hero and pictures of Wessel carried in solemn procession. Everyone waits for the Führer to appear. The murdered boy's mother keeps asking, "Where is Hitler?" But Hitler never shows up. He is spending the weekend with his half-niece, Geli Raubl, at his mountain retreat. She is squatting over Germany's "savior" while the Nazi martyr is solemnly laid to rest. Later the murdered boy's mother will write Hitler an indignant letter, which will go unanswered.

All the Nazi mythology, the Nazi trappings are cut from this same shoddy cloth. Because the bottom line is that Hitler is a fraud, an opportunist who believes in nothing but power for its own sake. He is the spirit of destruction. People may talk of his "mistake" in opening a second front against Russia in the east while he is still fighting Britain in the west. Or they may point to his "error" in senselessly declaring war on America while fighting the Russian colossus. His political advisers will deplore his treatment of the Slavic populations in the conquered territories—Why murder and torture them *now*? Why not wait until after the war?—because they know that the peasants are fed up with Stalin's harsh treatment and can be a great help to the Nazis in finishing off the Bolshevik regime. Stalin himself says of Hitler, "His problem is that he does not know when to stop."

But the truth is that he cannot do otherwise. Hitler and the force he has released, Nazism, can never stop devouring, conquering, seeking new enemies, setting up death camps wherever his armies are victorious. It can only be ended with Hitler's own death.

As Fegelein climbs up into the light to his execution, he passes a petty official coming down. With the official's arrival, the macabre death-wedding is ready to begin.

Eva Braun is in black silk, Hitler in a uniform. The secretaries, the Goebbelses, Bormann, the bodyguards solemnly stand in a semicircle to listen to the couple pledge their vows.

"Of Aryan descent, with no hereditary disease," Hitler murmurs, and the bride begins to sign "Eva Braun" but suddenly remembers and writes "Eva Hitler" instead, handing the pen to her groom, who scrawls "Adolf Hitler" and then, in the space provided for his father's name, fills in the discarded family name, "Schicklgruber."

There is a light supper, with reminiscences eventually slipping into the misery of the present. Hitler goes off to dictate his will—a repetition of all the lies and obsessive hatreds that have formed the message of his life. He and his bride retire to their bedroom, and it is then, on the last night in the bunker, as the Russians inexorably close in, that the others begin to party, dancing and drinking and laughing so loudly that at one point Hitler sends them a message to quiet down.

By the next night, Hitler will have shot himself in the

mouth; Eva Braun will have taken poison; and both their bodies will have been dragged up to the Chancellery garden, which is now filled with shattered stone swastikas and fallen marble columns. Below in the bunker, Goebbels and his wife and children are dying, along with two of the loyal generals, while everyone else is getting ready to escape. Some will make it through the Russian lines, some will not. At any rate, the secretaries have all been provided with poison capsules by Hitler—a parting gift—in case they find themselves in the hands of the barbarous Russians.

The beautiful secretary Traudl Junge goes into the Führer's room for a last look at the bed where Hitler has slept. A pool of dried blood stains the carpet near the couch on which he has shot himself. A whip Hitler liked to flourish and a pair of gray gloves lie on a chair near the door. She reaches out to take the gloves, to keep them as a memento, but *something* stops her, she doesn't know what.

Her hesitation sums up a dilemma the entire German nation will face in the future, because the gloves are in their way highly charged symbols: to put her hands into them is an act of complicity, of being hand-in-hand with the Führer, of admitting guilt; yet at the same time it is an act of hiding guilt, of covering over the traces like a gloved murderer. For the moment, however, the young secretary merely senses that she is in the presence of a dark riddle, so she turns and rushes into the hall, where the lights have begun to flicker as the generators stop working. The Russians could arrive at any moment, she realizes, and she joins a group of the "faithful" who have decided to try to flee Berlin. Using flashlights and candles they make their way up the bunker stairs—and out into the future, which holds various destinies for them: captivity in Russian prisons; trials in Nuremberg or in one of the de-Nazification courts set up throughout Germany; obscurity and exile in Latin American countries; or, for some, ease and honor in the new Germany that will rise from the ashes of the old.

Meanwhile, in the garden, the adjutants work quickly in the glare of the exploding bombs, dousing the bodies of Hitler and Eva with gasoline and setting them on fire. Finished with their grisly task, the men salute, then hurry to the doorway of the bunker and watch as the flames consume the body of their leader. And so in a matter of moments the former Master of Europe and all-powerful Führer is transformed by his final spectacle into a shattered skull and a heap of charred bones, thus fulfilling in death the plea from the Hebrew prayer, *Let all that is evil vanish like smoke.*

STALIN

I.   A VOCATION

One death is a tragedy. A million deaths are a statistic.
> —Joseph Stalin

Stalin knew everything; he directed everything; he *heard* everything: the lovemaking of a couple in bed, the leisurely conversations of his subordinates as they sat around their tables; the shrieks of agony in the Lubyanka. From his statues in the public squares to endless references to him in schoolbooks, he permeated the consciousness of 200 million Russians for three decades. He was inescapable, even after his death in 1953 and beyond. . . .

KIEV, 1991. A yellowing, flyblown photo, *Stalin at the Front During World War II,* looks down from the wall of a shabby apartment. It is a fake. Stalin never risked his life either before the revolution or after, saying that he preferred to live for the Cause rather than to die for it. Below the photo, an old woman wrapped in a black shawl sits telling lies about a vanished world. A young journalist listens to her skeptically, asking questions he never would have dared to ask just a few years before, a sign even more significant than the toppled statues of Lenin that the Communist regime is at an end.

How can the new generation understand that strange combination of idealism and cruelty at the heart of the Marxist revolution? The light and the darkness are inextricably mixed together, and it is only by seeing this that young Russians can come to terms with their history, violent, apocalyptic, visionary, depraved as it is.

"Yes, it is all over," the old woman says ruefully. "And now they will turn Joseph Vissarionovich [Stalin] into a monster, though at least he fought for some goal, on behalf of humanity!" She pauses, adding with a passionate quaver, "And what came of it?"

The old woman is bitter, and her bitterness is understandable given that her husband was Lavrentii Beria, head of the secret police from 1938 until Khrushchev had him arrested and executed in 1953, after Stalin's death. "Khrushchev was the first one to throw stones. About a year or so after Stalin died, there was some ceremony or other in Lenin's Mausoleum and that coarse peasant suddenly shouted, 'I can't stand the stench of Stalin's corpse in here!' The next day the Mausoleum was closed and they carried Stalin out and reburied him under the Kremlin wall. That was his end! A man who had ruled Russia for thirty years!"

The journalist asks her how Beria would have acted had he and not Khrushchev taken over after Stalin, but instead of answering directly, Mme. Beria changes the subject, describing how she met her husband, the patriotic fervor that had brought them together. Another story, though, a "love story" more typical of Stalin's time is told by those who knew her during that time. That version of their meeting has her coming to Beria to plead for her brother's life and Beria raping her in the police chief's private railway car. Afterward, Beria is about to throw her out when his sensuality is again aroused by her exotic beauty. Beria, usually blasé and surfeited with debauchery, is himself amazed by his reaction—What is so special about this girl? He takes her along with him and by the end of the trip decides to make her his wife. Her brother disappears forever in the torture chambers of the Lubyanka.

"Of course there were excesses, of course there were mistakes." Mme. Beria sighs. "But the times can't be judged by today's standards. You have to remember what Lenin taught: 'There is no morality outside the revolution!' We were encircled by enemies. The capitalists wanted to see us fail. In the beginning, the French, the British, even the Americans landed soldiers on Russian soil to support the Whites [the counter-revolutionaries]. The British executed twenty-six Bolshevik commissars! Twenty-six!

"Desperate times called for desperate measures— What? you don't think there were spies and wreckers and saboteurs even in the '30s? If Stalin told my husband that someone was guilty, then he *was* guilty. That's all there was to it. And it was up to Lavrentii to get a confession. It was his *duty*. Of course, some of his assistants went about it with too much zeal. Some weren't too bright, or had drinking problems, or worse.

"Which is to say, they were human. My husband passed an interrogation room one day and asked how things were going. 'He's a stubborn so-and-so! He's clammed up and hasn't said a word all afternoon,' his assistant complained, pointing to the prisoner, who was lying in a corner. But when Lavrentii looked at him, he saw the reason right away—he was dead, he'd been beaten to death." She laughs, shaking her head at the young journalist, who looks at her with horror.

But what does he hope to hear? Does he think that this ancient survivor will repudiate her youth? If anything, she must cling to it all the more fiercely now. Next to the photographic portrait of Stalin "at the front," the Berias' wedding picture still hangs overhead, a perfect symbol of the deceptive past. The bride, an exotic beauty, looks out at you with large dark eyes and a melancholy smile; Beria, with his dreamy expression, with his pince-nez and his sensual lips, resembles anything but the cold-blooded murderer he was.

Which was Beria's style throughout: poised, elegant, detached, a cool and contemplative figure. In fact, he seemed so completely civilized that all Russia sighed with relief when he replaced the evil dwarf Yezhov, a hysteric given to terrible rages, as head of the political police, the NKVD. In 1938 a new era had dawned, it was universally believed. Beria's star was in the ascendant and Yezhov was locked up in an asylum for the criminally insane, where he was discovered hanging from a bar of his cell with a placard around his neck proclaiming "I am shit." Thus the *Yezhovshchina,* the time of Yezhov, was brought to an end. The terror was over, people thought, not realizing that only the style of terror had changed, nothing more.

"Treason rests in every man," is Stalin's advice to Henryk Yagoda, who preceded Yezhov as head of the NKVD. "The only question is how deeply one has to probe to uncover it." (Later, when Yagoda is arrested and brought before a meeting of the Central Committee, he is jeered and heckled by Stalin's lackeys, who up until then had trembled before him. "I wish I had arrested you when I still had the power!" the tortured torturer shouts as he is dragged away to his death.)

In a sense it makes no difference who rules the slave empire of fourteen million men, women, and children worked to death or tortured to insanity in the NKVD prisons and concentration camps. From the first head of the secret police, the Polish aristocrat Dzerzhinsky, a Russianized convert to bolshevism who dies of a stroke after delivering a wildly hysterical attack on Stalin's "enemies" at a Party Congress; to Merzhinsky, an aesthete who likes to read out loud from the classics or play Tchaikovsky on the piano in his Lubyanka office—the prisoners could hear him on their way to execution; to Yagoda, the Kremlin pharmacist recruited by Stalin for his knowledge of subtle poisons and noxious gases; to the unbalanced Yezhov, whose diabolical cruelty surpasses description; to the clever, stylish Beria, without whose dynamic direction the Soviet atomic program would have taken years longer to achieve success, they are all mere ciphers. Because behind them all is the one man who called this nightmare into being, Stalin, the self-named man of steel.

Born Joseph Djugashvilli in a small town in Georgia in 1879, his first years were spent in a hovel that doubled as his cobbler father's workshop (and which in the 1940s Beria will enclose in a huge marble monument). The son of slaves, Stalin's father struggled to make a living as a shoemaker before finally losing what little he had through drunkenness. He then hired himself out as a laborer in a neighboring city, when he wasn't too drunk to work. Joseph's mother, unable to depend on her husband, supported herself and her son by cleaning houses and taking in sewing and washing at night.

Stalin was silent about his early years and those who "chattered" were liable to find themselves locked up in "isolators" for the rest of their lives, as was the case with some of his wife's relatives. Though Stalin never talked about his father, the circumstances of the father's life must have weighed heavily on the son's mind. The proverbial Russian expression "drunk as a shoemaker" was on Stalin's lips at crucial moments, most notably in a telegram he sent to Lenin during the Civil War, describing some Red officials he ordered shot at Tsaritsyn. Equally telling is his reference to a "poor shoemaker who lost his shop" in a speech he gave to the Party Congress. The shoemaker, who hopes one day to recover his workshop, is harshly criticized as having a petit bourgeois and not a revolutionary consciousness, despite his economic circumstances.

Though as a boy Stalin was something of a runt, with one arm shorter than the other, he was strong and managed to recover from an almost fatal attack of typhoid, developing into a wiry, determined, aggressive wrestler who dominated his young classmates. The story is told of him hurling a knife at his father who was beating his mother in a drunken rage, and then hiding with neighbors until his father left the house.

His only chance for a future was to do well enough in the church grammar school to be admitted to the Orthodox seminary in Tiflis, the Georgian capital. Daily, his mother prostrated herself in front of the icons with one fervent cry: "Let my son become a priest!" And her prayers were answered, at least this far: that the young Joseph was sharp-witted enough to succeed in winning a scholarship, his only chance of continuing his education. At the age of fourteen, therefore, he left his village and entered the theological seminary in Tiflis, where he was to be a student for the next five years.

The transition from the small town was a dramatic one. Tiflis was a half-European, half-Asiatic city with narrow, crooked lanes, bazaars and open stalls, noisy throngs of Persians, Armenians, Azerbaijanis, Arabs, and Turks, heat and dust, and the fortresslike Orthodox seminary, whose gates were locked at dusk on its students in their small dark cells.

The significance of the seminary was as much political as religious. Georgia, an ancient kingdom on the border of the Muslim and Christian worlds, was conquered by the tsars in the early nineteenth century who used the Church to try to Russianize the province. Afraid that a secular university would become a hotbed of Georgian nationalism, the tsarist authorities offered the seminary as an alternative, at the same time keeping a sharp watch on the students.

The young Stalin enters a world of spies planted at every turn to report the slightest gesture or comment that savors of impiety; rooms are searched at all hours for forbidden books. Stalin is caught more than once reading Hugo or de Maupassant and is punished with solitary confinement. Days are spent studying Old Church Slavonic and the liturgy, and faces are scrutinized during the hours of prayer to determine who is sincere—as Stalin will peer into the faces of his subordinates in later years, searching for treason. In short, the seminary's atmosphere is as stifling as it will be in Stalin's Russia, an ideal training ground for a future tyrant.

Those students with spirit, like Stalin, play cat-and-mouse with the monks and manage to augment the pious exercises with inquiries of a more dangerous kind. Stalin reads Darwin and Marx, steals away to meetings of the Mesame Dasy, a Georgian socialist group, and becomes a thorough-going atheist, all the while getting excellent grades in his strenuous theological studies, so that his scholarship is renewed year after year.

Strange to say, perhaps the most important lesson Stalin learns during this time, a lesson which helps him triumph in the power struggle after Lenin's death, is how to "read" a sacred text; that is, the art of interpretation, exegesis, hermeneutics. In both the seminary and the world of Marxist politics, all authority ultimately derives from texts. In the seminary it is scripture, of course, and in the Party, the writings of Marx become infallible dogma (Marx-Lenin by the 1920s).

In both Church and Party, though, the texts cry out for interpretation; that is, the text becomes a "pretext," which the interpreters use to assert their own authority. After all, deciding what is true doctrine and what is heresy or "deviation," to use Bolshevik terminology, is ultimately up to them. Thus Stalin will bludgeon his enemies with Marx, showing how their theoretical deviations make them dangerous "enemies of the people" who must be put to death.

Even those who abjectly "recant," such as the old Bolsheviks Zinoviev and Kamenev, will be shot in the purges of the '30s for having once held suspect positions. Bukharin, perhaps the most brilliant mind in the Party, bewildered, writes to Stalin from prison, "Why do you need me to die?" but dies without receiving an answer from his former comrade. There is no answer, none besides the official explanation: *You are a deviationist.* By the '30s, the time of the high terror, the more inexplicable the arrests, the more intense the terror. Friends and foes alike suffer. Stalin was never distracted by principles or doctrine. He always kept his eye on what was the real issue throughout: power.

Thus from the Church inquisitors Stalin learns how to use doctrine as a weapon, but he learns very little else. The formal course of study at the seminary, though strenuous, is so narrow as to be useless in terms of his intellectual development. The subjects he pursues on his own, in secret bouts of reading, are philosophy, economy, history, the ones that will matter in later years.

But his studies are sketchy at best. Stalin, though shrewd, even brilliant in some respects, will never equal the intellectual attainments of Lenin or Trotsky, both men from middle-class backgrounds, both formed from their youth by bourgeois culture, both with university educations. Stalin's ignorance is at the heart of both his strength and his weakness. He has gifts that can never be learned in the university, and deficiencies that result from never having studied in the university.

And he is intensely conscious of his flaws, hating and envying his contemporary, the Jew Trotsky, for his eloquence, his fame, his principles, his learning, and his popularity, especially with the army.

His attitude toward Lenin is a different matter. From the very beginning Stalin accepts the older man as a superior, taking Lenin as his master. If the monks repel the young Stalin, and if the Georgian socialists are too tame, too moderate to attract him, Lenin is a kindred spirit, fierce, implacable, ruthless. Unlike Stalin, though, Lenin is able to justify his ruthlessness with a deep knowledge of Marxist thought and of philosophy in general. Over the next two decades, Lenin will impose *his* vision of what the revolutionary Party will be, turning Marxism into Marxism-Leninism just as surely as Saint Paul put his stamp on the teachings of Jesus.

What is difficult to remember now, after the fact, is that Marxism did not necessarily have to take the form it did. There were other interpreters of Marx, Rosa Luxemburg, for example, who could have steered the movement in a different direction. But Lenin, with his skill in polemics, his fanatical persistence, his uncompromising idealism, his passion and his logic, ultimately defeated all opponents.

From his exile in Europe, Lenin publishes pamphlets, articles, books, learned treatises, and exhortations in the underground press in Russia. The young seminarian avidly consumes them, but soon he is chafing at the bit, ready to throw himself into revolutionary work and no longer able to put up with the pretense of piety. Openly showing his contempt for the authorities, he remains seated in the presence of the rector. "Do you know who is standing before you?" the rector asks, and the disciple of Lenin answers with an indifferent shrug, "Yes, a black speck."

Stalin leaves the seminary before finishing his final exams. He has embraced a dogma—but not a Christian one.

II. A QUESTION OF IDENTITY

PARIS, 1950. On a sweltering August day in an apartment decorated with tsarist memorabilia, a stylishly dressed man draws the curtains. Even though he is in Paris, the man, General Spiridovich, a former head of the tsarist political police, the Okhrana, practices caution. Wasn't Trotsky similarly safe in Mexico City when one of Stalin's agents, dressed in an Indian poncho and a wide-brimmed straw hat, stole upon him as he sat writing and drove an ice pick into the back of his skull? At that very moment, Trotsky was penning one of his bitter invectives against Stalin, invoking the judgment of history on the Soviet tyrant and comparing him to Nero. His blood was splattered across the page and the sentence broken off.

Thus Stalin answered Trotsky's famous eloquence with an eloquence of his own. Other critics of the *Khozyain,* "the Boss," will similarly disappear over the years or be silenced by threats to the lives of relatives still in Russia.

So our general may be excused if he looks over his shoulder before proceeding with the business at hand. A sleuth, hired by an "interested party," has come to see him with a fantastic letter whose authenticity he is trying to confirm. The detective is aware that it contains information about the young Stalin that could cause an international sensation, and thus he has gone to great lengths.

So far, though, all of the detective's leads have been dead ends—literally. Stalin has been careful to cover his tracks. Everyone who knew him in the years just after he left the seminary is either dead or smart enough to remain silent. Not even Abel Yenukidze, the godfather of Stalin's children, has been spared. Likewise Ordzhonikidze, a garrulous, high-spirited comrade from the early days: his death is announced as a heart attack and Stalin even attends his funeral. Likewise Kamo, that half-mad daredevil the young Stalin trained to rob banks for the Cause. Kamo will be run down by a truck one day in the streets of the Georgian capital in an "accident" typical of the '30s, when circumspection, not courage or wildness, is required. The list is endless.

The detective therefore has turned to Okhrana agents for information, men in the service of the late tsar who followed Stalin's career and are therefore in a unique position. Months of searching have finally led the detective to ex-general Spiridovich, a man deeply sympathetic to his mission. Opening a locked cabinet, the general takes out a gift from long ago, a silver decanter, and shows it to the detective. The signatures of his fellow Okhrana officers are engraved on it, along with some sentimental sayings.

But only one signature is important now, that of *Eremin,* the writer of the letter, which is a report on the young Stalin. As the detective compares the signature on the letter with the one on the decanter he smiles: they are a perfect match.

It is a priceless document. In fact, it will be bought by the Tolstoy Foundation in New York for a small fortune, justifying the "interested party's" expense. But its real significance is political, not monetary. Eremin wrote it on the occasion of the transfer of the prisoner Joseph Dju- gashvilli, also known as Stalin, to a penal colony in Siberia. After describing the prisoner's activities in Georgia and the Transcaucasus, he details the help Stalin gave the tsarist police. "He [Stalin] provided the chief of the Tiflis Provin- cial Gendarme Administration with valuable denunciatory information when he was arrested in 1906. In 1908 the chief of the Baku Okhrana Section received a series of in- telligence reports from him, and afterward, upon Stalin's arrival in Petersburg, he became an agent of the Petersburg Okhrana section. His work was distinguished by accuracy, but was fragmentary. . . . I am informing you, dear sir, of the above for personal consideration in the conduct of op- eration work."

The damning letter remained in the Okhrana files until the first phase of the revolution. When Kerensky's soldiers arrested the officer in charge of the Okhrana's files, they found him burning a large batch of secret re- ports. Still and all, after a brief interrogation, they released him, and the officer managed to escape with the Eremin letter to Shanghai, where he found employment as a chauffeur. And sold this potential bombshell to an "inter- ested party."

For a variety of reasons, however, the bombshell did not explode until 1956, after Stalin had been dead for three years. In 1956 it finally came to the attention of Stalin's first English-speaking biographer, Don Levine, who published a sensational article about it in *Life* maga- zine, followed by an equally ill-considered short book, *Stalin's Great Secret*. These exposés were indignantly repu- diated by Khrushchev and the Communist Party. The So- viet leadership did not want to disillusion the rank and file Communists with such cynical revelations. Stalin was for an entire Soviet generation an idealized father, whom even many prisoners in the gulag sincerely mourned.

Paulina Molotov, for example, the Jewish wife of the foreign minister, is imprisoned for five years in isolators and torture chambers during Stalin's last, anti-Semitic, purge. Yet she will faint with grief when she hears that Stalin is dead, even though it means that her ordeal is at an end. "He saved our nation during World War II! He destroyed the Fifth Column with his purges!" she is to say later when anyone attacks Stalin. And her response, shockingly enough, is not an isolated one but is typical of millions of Soviet citizens. Something like mass hysteria results, even in the prison camps, when Stalin's death is announced. Which is to say that the average citizen's fear of Stalin was mixed with love.

And so the Soviets scoff at the letter and call it a hoax. In a final, complicated twist to the story, it turns out that the letter *is* a hoax, though its contents are almost certainly true. That is, the letter is evidence forged to prove facts which are true but unprovable.

An expert is called in, who can find no fault with Eremin's signature: its perfection as a forgery is a mystery. However, the expert discovers many other discrepancies which lead him to uncover the fraud. Perhaps the most telling is that the letter is typed on an old beat-up machine; the print is of the sort produced by keys that had been used for a number of years. But the letter is dated 1913, and the Adler Company first manufactured typewriters using the Cyrillic alphabet a few months earlier. If Eremin had actually typed the letter in 1913, it would have to have been typed on a new machine, which it was not.

Perhaps the Okhrana officer in charge of Stalin's file typed the letter after he fled to Shanghai, taking a stock of Okhrana stationery with him. It is even possible that he had seen a real letter about Stalin in the files which he destroyed, and that he later reproduced it from memory. Apart from the letter, though, the circumstantial facts of Stalin's early career point to his being an informer who received special privileges and money from the tsarist authorities.

Time and again he avoids arrest, until his comrades get suspicious, at which point he is arrested and given a light sentence, or escapes shortly thereafter. *Somehow,* he has no difficulty leaving and reentering the country for meetings of the Party in Prague and London, or for special conferences with Lenin in Vienna. Most significant, though, is the fact that that rival comrades in the revolutionary underground are swiftly arrested at critical junctures.

The history of the letter is symbolic of the history of the Marxist revolution and the seventy-year-long Communist experiment, with its many reversals and ironies, its lies-within-truths and its truths-within-lies. If it is a difficult business to unravel on a simple, factual level, on a psychological level it is even more complex. For Stalin is a mystery-within-an-enigma, (as Churchill will describe Russia during World War II). If he becomes Lenin's fanatical follower after leaving the seminary, he also has an eye on the main chance. Jealous of and engaged in power struggles with his revolutionary comrades, he plays every card he has in his hand. And if that hand includes some unscrupulous dealings with the tsarist police, so be it. That is his way. To be shocked is to be naive about how Stalin attained power and kept it. If he had been more principled, he would have been the one with the ice pick thrust into his skull, not Trotsky.

That was the spirit of the times. Masks were worn not just by Stalin but by many of the players in revolutionary Russia, masks which, as in the fairy tale, *became* the face of the wearer, whose identity is thus undiscoverable.

Perhaps it is the memory of his own treachery that makes Stalin so watchful. In power, he executes hundreds of thousands not because they are disloyal but because they *may* be disloyal. Thirty-six thousand officers of the Red Army are executed; the flower of the army is destroyed on the eve of World War II. All the *millions of* Russian soldiers taken prisoner by the Nazis are imprisoned again for years when they return home, most to be worked to death. The figures are mind-boggling. "Why didn't they fight to the death? How could they allow themselves to have been taken prisoner?" Stalin asks, ignoring the fact that his blunders were largely responsible for their having been captured.

In keeping with this view, Stalin lets his son Yakov die in a Nazi prisoner of war camp rather than exchange a single German soldier for him. There exists a pathetic photo of Yakov in his death agonies: after months of torture and special ridicule, he flings himself onto the electric barbwire fence. But why should his father lift his finger to help a traitor? What's more, Stalin arrests his son's wife as the wife of a traitor, of a man who has not died fighting but who has "allowed himself" to be captured.

All this is in the future, of course. But the young Stalin's double-dealing is all the more remarkable in light of such harshness. How did he excuse his own behavior to himself? The more one contemplates the contradictions of his life, the harder it is to understand the motives for his behavior. There are layers of concealment, and it is difficult to define Stalin's real nature, his real relationship to Marxist belief, to his comrades, his heroes, his victims.

Even in his most characteristic attitude, his class hatred, there is ambiguity. Coming from the working class himself, he had no illusions about workers or peasants. He did not romanticize them as the bourgeois Lenin tended to; in fact, part of Stalin's appeal for Lenin was that Stalin came from the working class.

Organizing the railroad workers in Tiflis, the oil workers in Baku, the young Stalin continually repeated the Bolshevik line: the workers must accept orders from above. Left to themselves they might bargain for economic benefits, but they would never arrive at a revolutionary position, they would never demand a fundamental change in the ownership of the means of production.

The paradox is, then, Stalin's fundamental distrust of the workers at the same time that he is making a revolution in their name. And the fact of the matter is that the leading figures of this so-called workers' revolution are drawn from the educated, bourgeois class.

"Gravedigger of the revolution!" Trotsky hurls the insult, what Marx called Napoleon, at Stalin during their furious debates after Lenin's death. "You have betrayed the ideals of the revolution!"

"Mass murderer!" his second wife shouts at him just before her suicide.

On each of these occasions, Stalin disdains answering his accusers. But if he had, the line he would have taken would have been that he was "destroying the revolution" in order to save it. It is a logic similar to the one espoused by Franco, who announces during the Spanish Civil War that he will kill every single Spaniard if he has to, in order to save Spain. If Stalin temporarily transgresses Marxist ideals, it is out of necessity. This is his logic, from his earliest days as an informer for the tsarist officials, to his great gamble in 1939 when he completely violates Marxist doctrine to sign a pact with Hitler, the archenemy of communism.

What is behind the mask at such moments? Outwardly, Stalin is more gracious and patient with the Nazis than he has been with any other group, either foreign or Russian. He allows Hitler's personal photographer to take all the close-ups he likes. (Hitler has instructed the man to get good shots of Stalin's ears, he wants to make sure his fellow dictator has no Jewish blood in him.)

Again and again, Stalin's outward actions directly contradict his professed beliefs. He drinks with, toasts, embraces the Nazis—together they carve up Poland—just as in his very un-Marxist way he will let millions of Russian peasants starve in the '30s to implement farm collectivization. "In the countryside they have taken to cannibalism," his wife will plead with him, but this supposed leader of the workers and peasants will do nothing. In fact, he is even more suspicious of the peasants than he is of the workers; he punishes their pathetic attempts to keep a cow, a vegetable patch, a sack of grain for themselves, with death.

Stalin's answer to all reproaches can be summed up in one word: survival.

So the question then becomes: Survival of the revolution or his own personal survival?

And the answer Stalin gives, if not in so many words, is: I *am* the revolution.

III.   THE UNWILLING STARGAZER

Dead men have no problems.

> —Stalin's remark, in 1919, on hearing
> that there was a problem with the
> evidence against some court-
> martialed Red soldiers. The men
> were shot.

TIFLIS, GEORGIA, 1901. If a visitor made his way to the highest point in the city at night, he would come upon a strange sight. There, in the Astronomical Observatory, a young man with a swarthy, pockmarked face, thick black hair, and an absorbed expression sits over a dog-eared copy of Marx's *Das Kapital*. The silence of the night is broken only by the sound of "Allahu-akhbar" from a nearby mosque or sometimes by the chanting of Russian monks holding vigil in the cemetery below. From time to time the young man pauses impatiently in his reading to peer through the huge telescopes and jot down the positions of the stars.

It is the only regular job that Stalin will ever hold, a

night job, well suited to his needs at the time. It permits him to spend his days at secret Party meetings or with factory and railroad workers, translating Marx into their rough idiom, which is his as well. Addressing small groups of workers while a partner looks out for the police, Stalin speaks haltingly, even when using Georgian. His manner is reserved, stiff, inhibited. He has none of the fiery passion of Lenin or Trotsky; it is only in private conversation, among comrades, that his cruelty finds expression in mordant, cynical remarks.

His style is the opposite of Hitler's frantic raving; yet his quiet charisma is in its way just as powerful. When he gives his first speech to a larger crowd, at the May Day celebrations in Tiflis, his train of thought is somewhat confused, mixing the failure of the wine harvest with Georgian national aspirations and the exploitation of the workers. Yet his presence, his authority, wins over those who listen.

Still, the audience is a small one compared to the international forum commanded by such figures as Lenin or Trotsky. In fact, by the time of the 1917 revolution Stalin will be unknown outside Russia and recognized *in* Russia only by a handful of comrades, although he has worked in the underground for years.

It galls him, but it is a strength. His enemies underestimate him. The "superior" Trotsky will mockingly call him "the Party's great unrecognized mediocrity," while Zinoviev and Kamenev, two other Party luminaries at the time of Lenin's death, imagine that they can use Stalin for their own ends in the ensuing power struggle. Even Lenin, who appreciates his strength and determination, never imagines that this Georgian peasant will be his successor. Stalin quietly gathers power among the provincial leaders, the rank and file. He leaves Trotsky and Bukharin at center stage while behind the scenes he prepares. He knows how to wait.

In 1901 Stalin is on the threshold of his new life. From his eyrie, the Astronomical Observatory, he can hear bombs exploding in the center of the city. There are cries from a panic-stricken crowd: soldiers lie bleeding to death in the square while young men, boys no older than fourteen and fifteen, leap into the carnage and seize a shipment of money being sent to the Central Bank in Moscow. In a matter of moments they have fled, leaving the people to their horror, the police to their rage, and the ex-seminarian to his stars. No one suspects that Stalin has planned the brutal and efficient operation; not even the director of the observatory, who for the next month will sleep on a mattress stuffed with millions of rubles (money which will be sent abroad to finance the revolutionary Party).

For his part, Stalin will remain silent on the subject, even when he is in power. The holdups and extortions he practices on the local merchants are a sordid business; probably the reason for his reticence is that they show him in a criminal light too close to his nature for comfort.

In fact, during the years that follow, when Stalin spends varying amounts of time in tsarist prisons, it is with the criminals he associates, not the politicals. When not lying brooding in his cell—or studying Esperanto, which he thinks will be the language of the future, he drinks and swaps stories with the forgers, thieves, rapists, and murderers who become his prison friends.

The politicals, with their garrulous discussions of the future Utopia, bore Stalin, but his eyes light up when he hears that a new arrival is in prison for something "real." "Hey, chief!" his voice can be heard over the others at mealtime. "How about some more bread?" And he gets it, along with whatever else he wants, including liquor. Drinking is a habit he picked up in the cradle, he is given to saying, because his father used to dip his finger into wine and put it in the baby's mouth.

His behavior in jail forecasts the methods he will use throughout his life, a mix of cunning and brutality. The prison criminals can get him what he wants, but what can the politicals offer? His interest in the other revolutionaries extends only this far: to play them off against each other, to dominate the weak and destroy the strong. More than once he will get rid of those he considers enemies by starting a rumor that the man is an informer. The hapless victim is beaten to death. More than once he will sow the seeds of dissension between two factions in the prison, practicing the kind of politics that will become his specialty.

Up until the observatory is raided by the police, Stalin keeps a foot in two worlds. His papers are in order, he is "legitimate," and he is a revolutionary. After the raid, during which a large stash of his revolutionary literature is uncovered, he goes into hiding, living under one assumed identity after another from 1901 until the revolution in 1917.

These years are a cycle of secret revolutionary activity: arrest, escape, a return to the underground, and re-arrest. And it is at some point in this cycle that he strikes the cynical bargain with the secret police that Captain Eremin is supposed to have written about. It is not likely that Stalin worked for them for more than a few years. Once he rose in Party ranks he would have risked being exposed.

For the few years it lasted, however, Stalin's Machiavellian bargain is useful. The secret police are interested in recruiting informers and agent provocateurs, men who will bring the revolutionaries out of hiding and into open confrontation with the authorities. The monarchists reason that such clashes will lead to arrests and executions, thus purging society of its radical elements.

Stalin also wants violent confrontation, but for different reasons. His reasoning, following Lenin's, is that the government's violence will only strengthen the Party. Every witness to scenes of brutal Cossacks on horseback whipping students and workers will win converts, create martyrs, and like a stone thrown in water, have a ripple effect. In Tiflis, in Batum, on the Black Sea, in Baku, on the Caspian, he incites riots, strikes, and sabotage in the oil fields and railway plants. In Baku alone, he fills the prisons to overflowing and then stirs up more than thirty thousand workers to demonstrate for their jailed comrades. His shift from Georgia to Azerbaijan is a necessity: a comrade's court, members of the Party who decide all internal disputes, expels him for creating dissension and hatred among its members in his effort to dominate them.

"My two years among the oil workers of Baku hardened me," he was to say later of his work in the Transcaucasus, and indeed he *is* hardened—to the suffering of others. He takes care that he is not in the thick of the battle when the Cossacks arrive. Another advantage of being an informer.

The police arrest him from time to time, of course, but he makes sure that it is never on a capital charge. When he finally breaks with the Okhrana, the shoe will be on the other foot. His longest stint in jail will be the result of a comrade's treachery, the suave, charming, double-dealing Bolshevik Roman Malinowsky, who will be executed by Lenin after the revolution. Later, in a revealing aside, Stalin reflects that it was a pity Lenin executed Malinowsky: "As if it were only a question of death . . ." Because in the

warped world of Stalin's prisons and work camps, death is
a reward.

THE YEAR 1909, Baku, a port city of some 200,000 souls
on the Caspian Sea whose coast is dotted with oil towers.
The workers, Persians and Turks, Armenians and Geor-
gians, Tatars and Azerbaijanis, become desperate, and the
harsh conditions of their existence make them ripe for violence, for crime or revolution.

The impending chaos is described in a long, confidential cable. Delivered to an elderly count seated at cards in
a casino on the French Riviera, it reads like a message
from another world. The count, Vorontsov-Dashkov, one
of the richest men in tsarist Russia, is summoned from re-
tirement to be vice regent for the Transcaucasus.

"I have no wish to end my days as a hangman," he says
despondently, throwing down his cards. But he dutifully
starts for Georgia the same day, traveling through a land of
vineyards and medieval fortresses to take up his position in
the huge vice regent's palace in Tiflis. Wearily, with little
belief in the ability of the monarchy to survive, he turns to
the old strategy of divide and conquer. Secretly he arms
the more moderate Mensheviks and turns on the Bolsheviks in the midst of revolutionary disorders complicated
by the ethnic hatred between Armenians and Muslims.
Stalin is swept up in the round of arrests ordered by the
vice regent.

The old count orders a permanent gallows to be
erected in the Bailov Prison, a two-storied fortress at the
end of a barren stretch of land that juts out into the
Caspian Sea. During the day, the inmates are allowed to
wander the corridors and lounge about the courtyard.
Although the authorities make no distinction between the

politicals and the common criminals, the two groups keep to themselves, with the politicals arguing social theory in the very shadow of the gallows. This is typical of the prisons in tsarist Russia, which become the "universities of the revolution." It is the one place where open political discussion is tolerated, since the penalty has already been paid.

Night after night, however, when "school" is over, the prison echoes with the anguished cries of men being dragged off to midnight executions. The sound of their struggles makes sleep impossible. For everybody, that is, except Stalin, who is awakened not by the cries but by the silence that follows.

GORI, GEORGIA, 1907. Having escaped from prison, Stalin marries a simple village girl from the town where he was born. Her father and brothers are revolutionaries, so the wedding is also an occasion for Party members to gather and for business to go forward under cover of the festivities. The girl is beautiful, silent, simple, apolitical and religious. She treats Stalin like a god. During their few years of marriage she will spend her nights together with his mother lighting candles before the icons and praying for his safety. She bears Stalin a son, Yakov, and then dies young, of tuberculosis. At her funeral Stalin says in a rare outburst of feeling, "With her die all my human feelings." He gives their young son to her brother to raise. He himself has no home, no life outside the revolution.

But that is all in the future. At the wedding, Stalin for once is uncomplicated: a man in love. The relatives drink and dance in a traditional round. How can they know that when the groom achieves supreme power he will turn on his brother-in-law whose glass is raised now in a wedding toast? In the 1930s, he will demand that his brother-in-law confess his guilt as a traitor and would-be assassin. The man will protest his innocence and Stalin will have him tortured. But even under torture, he insists that he is no traitor. Finally Stalin sends word: "Confess and I will let you go. Otherwise, I will have you shot."

"The trees die standing," the condemned man says as he is taken away.

"I didn't think he was so proud," Stalin says on reading the report, and shrugs.

Stalin's few trips abroad when he is in the underground, to London, to Prague, to Helsinki, to Vienna, are made either to attend Party Congresses or to work with Lenin, who remains in exile until the revolution. The relationship between the two dissimilar men deepens. Lenin is impressed by Stalin's competence in practical matters, the massiveness and violence of the workers' demonstrations in the Transcaucasus, the fact that Stalin flinches at nothing in advancing the Bolshevik cause.

Stalin is the real thing, a revolutionary from the working class. And since he is, Lenin forgives him his rudeness, his surliness, and trusts his judgment, even helping him to produce the one credential he lacks for prominence in the party: a piece of theoretical writing. When the two meet in Prague, Lenin asks his protégé to write an article on the role Great Russia plays vis-à-vis the many ethnic groups scattered throughout the Russian Empire, the so-called nationalities question.

Apart from making suggestions for the article and refining Stalin's style, Lenin's choice of subject matter will give Stalin a power base in the future revolutionary government. The nationalities question is a problem that

Stalin, as a Georgian, comes to with firsthand knowledge and one that will be of central importance when the Russian Empire is transformed into the Soviet "Union." After the revolution, Stalin joins Lenin's politburo as commissar of nationalities, a position he will jockey into one of supreme power through that combination of brutality and cunning which is his unique gift. Just before his death Lenin will realize, with a cry of horror, that his "wonderful Georgian," as he had described Stalin in a letter, is inhuman, a beast, a monster. But by then it is too late.

During these first years, however, from 1901 until the revolution in 1917, the two revolutionaries share a long honeymoon. If the beast shows his claws, it is to Lenin's enemies, to counter-revolutionaries and adversaries in the party alike. In fact, this relationship, this marriage between the intellectual and the peasant, can be seen as one that sums up a hundred years of revolutionary history. It is symbolic of the role the Russian intelligentsia played in bringing about the brutalities of the revolution.

Dostoyevsky understood this. In his great novel *The Brothers Karamazov,* the brilliant Ivan teaches the half-witted peasant-servant that "Since there is no immortality [of the soul], everything is permitted." Thus the intellectual Ivan becomes the vicarious agent for the murder that is committed.

Like Ivan Karamazov, Lenin represents generations of Russian political intellectuals striving toward freedom with an ardor that admits no ethical or moral restraints. Perhaps it is the extremity of tsarist repression that makes them so radical, so desperate; it is no accident that the word "nihilism" is coined in Russia. There is a destructive, all-annihilating quality about Russian political radicalism from the early Decembrist movement in the 1820s to Nachaev's mid-nineteenth-century writings—

revolutionary catechism—to the anarchist Prince Kropotkin, at the turn of the century, who loathes politics, religion, and authority of any kind and only honors "the sacred instinct of revolution."

Nachaev (1847–1882) writes in his *Revolutionary Catechism,* "The revolutionary is a doomed man. He can have no friendship or attachment. . . . He should not hesitate to destroy any position, any place or any man in the world. The filthy social order can be split up into several categories—the first category comprises those who can be condemned to death without delay."

Although Lenin is a more sophisticated thinker than such predecessors, he is no less fanatic and no less deficient in ethical understanding. It is legitimate to blame Lenin in exile, writing in his study, for Stalin's torture chambers twenty years later because Lenin bears the moral responsibility for every drop of blood spilled by the latter—as do Trotsky and Bukharin and the whole company of Marxist ideologues.

Take Lenin at his best, bathed in sweat, his face aglow with inspiration (as his wife, Krupskaya, rapturously describes him). He is passionate about philosophy. During his exile he once holed up in a Paris library for two weeks and refused to meet a delegation of revolutionaries who had come on urgent business: he was busy working out a treatise on an obscure problem of doctrine. So it would be typical to represent him in his Paris library reading from Marx, his fellow "prophet," whom he resembles in breadth of learning. Or perhaps he is raging against injustice in one of his fiery pamphlets.

Next, with Lenin's voice in our ears proclaiming high-sounding socialist principles—or better still, with Lenin expounding the abstract, difficult philosophical passages he admired in Hegelian phenomenology, in Comte's empiri-

cism—imagine Stalin's Lubyanka Prison, where men and women are being strapped to tables. Their teeth are kicked out; they are forced to stand in vats of urine, or stare at two-thousand-watt lightbulbs, or sit on hot pipes until their buttocks are burned through. Their genitals are lashed with wet towels, needles are stabbed through the back of the neck until the spinal cord is injured and convulsions begin. Pregnant women are kicked to death in front of their husbands, children are slowly murdered in front of their mothers. After such horrors, the high, intellectual forehead of that prophet of the revolution, Lenin, preaching to a fallen humanity, can only fill us with revulsion.

EASTERN SIBERIA, SUBPOLAR REGION, 1914-1917. With the onset of World War I, Stalin remains in the penal colony to which he has been sentenced. His special relationship with the police has long since been terminated. An escape is too risky, because during the war the authorities, under martial law, shoot all escapees.

More than any revolutionary propaganda, the war exposes the weakness and incompetence of the tsarist regime. Russia is fifty years behind the West industrially, and its administration is pathetic. Soldiers are sent to the front without boots, let alone ammunition. Against the German war machine, Russia can only throw her masses of humanity to be cut to bits. The carnage, however, has the effect of saving Paris. Fighting a war on two fronts, the Germans must withdraw troops from the western front to fight in Russia.

"The peasants are voting with their feet," Lenin exults, noting the massive desertions. He knows that sooner or later his slogan, "Bread, Land, and Peace," will be irresistible, if not authentically Marxist, because to the peasants the promise of land runs against the notion of collective property. It a concession to reality, though, the first of many concessions Lenin, and after him Stalin, will be forced to make, since the peasants are land hungry and since the population is still largely rural.

"Papa, the villages are getting empty," Rasputin warns the tsar. But Nicholas II is deaf to warnings and fights on in a war that the simple people of Russia, the workers and the soldiers, cannot understand.

Meanwhile, Stalin fishes and hunts and broods. During the summer, the mosquitoes are so numerous that, one prisoner records in a journal, they sting a cow to death.

A net of tarred horsehair over his head, half buried in mud for relief from the insects, Stalin reads history, economics, political theory. However difficult life is in the Siberia of the tsars, it is nothing compared to what he will create in his arctic work camps. Under Stalin, men, women, and children will be forced to build canals or mine gold and minerals without proper clothes in the winter, sometimes standing up to their thighs in cold water until they lose all feeling in their legs, and lashed to death under the bored and sadistic scrutiny of the guards. In the Siberia of the tsars it is the endless monotony of nature that oppresses the exiles; the separation from family and friends, the isolation; the darkness in winter, the cold, the howling of wolves, the endless snow, the armies of cockroaches so numerous that they swarm over the beds and faces of the prisoners.

From time to time there are love affairs. When a commandant is lenient, he lets "his" prisoners visit the neighboring settlement for variety, which means covering hundreds of miles by dogsled over frozen wastes. Withdrawn, silent, and reclusive, Stalin keeps mainly to himself. There is a famous painting of Stalin during his Siberian exile, called *Stalin Reading a Letter from Lenin*. Reproductions were to be found in every schoolhouse in Soviet Russia, though such a letter was never written.

Stalin, however, *will* write a letter from Siberia, but it will not have a political theme. He asks a friend, a Mme. Alliluyeva, a woman with whom he has had a brief affair some years before, for pictures of nature, of flowers and trees and fields. He needs them, he says, to relieve the unbearable bleakness of his life. It is the only such letter he will write.

IV.   THE GIFT OF SILENCE

**If Krupskaya doesn't shut her mouth we will have
to get someone else to be Lenin's widow.**
                    —Stalin

ST. PETERSBURG, 1917. The revolution catches Lenin by
surprise. Russia is in chaos and the tsar abdicates suddenly.
Upon hearing the news in Siberia, and freed from the
penal colony, Stalin sets out at once for St. Petersburg, the
first Bolshevik leader to arrive in the capital.

The provisional government vows to continue the
war. From exile, Lenin calls the war a capitalist battle over
markets and colonies, and quoting Marx, he calls on the
workers of the world to unite in an international revolution. Again and again he repeats his slogan—Bread, Land,
Peace! German government officials decide to use Lenin
for their own purposes. They help him return to Russia,
arranging for him to travel through Germany in a sealed,
windowless train, inspiring Churchill's remark that the
kaiser, wanting to destroy his enemy, introduced the bacillus of bolshevism into Russia.

Every Soviet citizen has seen photos of Stalin greeting

Lenin upon his return and Soviet schoolbooks give accounts of the two leaders meeting at Finland Station. But it is a meeting that never occurred. The photos are doctored, the eyewitness accounts are manufactured, lies to show Stalin as having played a bigger part in the revolution than he did.

The truth is that Stalin was wary of greeting his mentor when he returned. There was no way of knowing how the moderate provisional government would react. Lenin, after all, was committed to ending the war and to establishing a communist state. The leaders of the provisional government, Prince Lvov and Kerensky, were liberals committed to continuing the war and establishing a democratic republic. If Stalin had been in Kerensky's place, he would have had Lenin arrested and executed. And as always, he projected his own ruthlessness onto others, in this case Kerensky, expecting the worst of him.

Thus the glorious, emotional, often described meeting took place several days later in the offices of *Pravda,* with no glory and very little emotion except for Lenin's rebuking Stalin for having published some articles not to his liking.

The crisis in Russia, however, is simply too much for the provisional government. Bolshevik propaganda has spread through the army, with Lenin and Trotsky calling on the soldiers to murder their officers and desert. There is a premature effort on the part of the Bolsheviks to seize power. The government calls for Lenin to turn himself in and stand trial. Stalin has been staying at the home of the same Mme. Alliluyeva who had sent him nature pictures in Siberia (she is now married and has two young daughters) and he hides Lenin at the Alliluyevs'. In a moment of tense comedy, Stalin acts as Lenin's barber, shaving his famous goatee to help disguise him. The danger to the Bolshevik

leader is short-lived, however, and the provisional government falls after less than a year in power, its only defenders members of a woman's brigade who bravely try to
hold the Winter Palace against overwhelming odds.

Kerensky escapes by flying the American flag on a military vehicle, and Lenin quickly comes out of hiding to
lead the new Bolshevik government. Stalin, named commissar of nationalities, gets one of the Alliluyev girls, the
sixteen-year-old Nadezhda, work as Lenin's secretary. She
is beautiful, her father is an old Georgian revolutionary,
and she is in love with Stalin.

The fact that Stalin is thirty-nine and she is sixteen,
that he is a hardened revolutionary just returned from
years in prison, that his closest comrades complain of his
being cruel and dominating, does not augur well for their
happiness. It is difficult to say when they actually become
lovers; many revolutionary couples formed attachments
without actually bothering with marriage certificates until
the first children came. According to the Soviet sexual
code, Nadezhda is too young to be living with Stalin, but
sexual codes are the last concern of a society that has just
been ripped apart by revolution and is in the midst of a
World War—indeed, at the time the Bolsheviks take
power, the Germans are occupying a vast area of Russian
territory.

There are those who argue against surrendering to the
Germans. A radical faction protests that the Communists
must fight to the last man and die as the heroes of the Paris
Commune did in 1848, leaving an example to history. But
Lenin is far too practical for that. Over the wireless, he orders the commander in chief of the Russian armies, General Donnikon, to surrender to the Germans.

Donnikon refuses. In what is probably the most dramatic promotion made in military history, something

more like being catapulted from a cannon than promoted, Lenin makes a certain Ensign Krylenko the new commander in chief on the spot and orders him to Mogilev to take over from Donnikon. After his disgrace, Donnikon, trying to leave Mogilev, is beaten to death at the train station by a mob of soldiers turned revolutionaries.

Such random violence is a sign of impending anarchy, of a breakdown of morale, Lenin understands, and assigns Trotsky to check it. Trotsky wins fame by transforming the Red Army from a pillaging ragtag mob into a disciplined fighting force. The fiery orator turns out to be a skilled organizer and strategist. But when Stalin comes to rewrite history, he will take credit for Trotsky's achievements just as he has removed Trotsky's face from the historical photo at the Finland Station and replaced it with his own.

In later years, Stalin obsessively erases the fact that his role in the revolution was a secondary one. It is more than propaganda: He himself cannot accept the fact that his skills are political, not military. His genius is for imposing order in a fragmented society. It is only in the most desperate hours of World War II, when the Nazis are at the gates of Moscow, that he openly accepts dictation from a military man, General Zhukov. But once the danger is past, his meddling begins again, to the detriment of the conduct of the war.

Similarly, during the Civil War, which follows the revolution, Stalin's contribution is mainly a political one. The Bolsheviks have repudiated the national debt; withdrawn from World War I; broken with their former allies, Great Britain, France, and America; and shot the tsar, Nicholas II, together with his empress and their five children and thrown their bodies down a mine shaft. "Now *they* will know there is no going back," Trotsky remarks. But *they* are *determined* to go back, *they* being the counterrevolutionary or "White" armies under Baron Wrangel and Admiral Kolchak, aided by French, British, and American forces hostile to the idea of a communist revolution.

The survival of the revolution hangs by a thread. Lenin sends his closest collaborators to the various collapsing fronts. In the northwest, the Whites have gotten to within a few miles of Leningrad (St. Petersburg). In the south, they are less than 150 miles from Moscow. It is vital to save the city of Tsaritsyn if Moscow is not to starve; grain from the south must travel north on Tsaritsyn's railroad. But the food shipments have stopped; the Whites are besieging the city, and the Reds in control are divided among themselves.

Stalin is sent to Tsaritsyn, where he telegrams back to Lenin that he will spare neither himself nor others. The fighting is fierce and the execution of wavering revolutionaries is summary. Amidst the carnage, Stalin makes love to his sixteen-year-old bride—it is their honeymoon— and then he returns to the black barge on the Volga where night after night he holds "military" trials of the Red officers, after which, invariably, the bodies of the accused are thrown into the river. Within a short time order is restored; the food shipments resume, and Tsaritsyn, to be renamed Stalingrad in the future, is saved.

But Stalin's success during the Civil War is only partial; he has been expending at least as much energy on undermining Trotsky, the war commissar and Lenin's heir apparent, as he has on fighting the Whites. He scrawls "To be ignored" on Trotsky's orders and encourages the commanders he trusts, such as Voroshilov and Budenny, his favorites, to be insubordinate to the "Jewish" war commissar.

Cleverly, Stalin seizes on an issue he knows is particularly unpopular with the regular soldiers, the use of former tsarist officers in the new Red Army Trotsky has organized. Trotsky's position is that these officers can play an important role in achieving a Red victory, arguing that they are like the scattered stones from a destroyed palace, which can now be used to build a revolutionary structure.

The rank and file hate the idea of serving under former imperial officers and Stalin sides with them, adding an element of anti-Semitism to the quarrel by remarking that in the old days the soldiers served a Romanov but now they serve an "Abramanov," that is, Trotsky, who was born with the Jewish name Lev Bronstein.

At first Lenin sides with Stalin. The idea of using ex-tsarist officers is abhorrent to him. But then Trotsky counters that without the forty thousand military experts from the old regime, the new army will be a shambles. During the fighting, Trotsky admits, there are cases of these ex-tsarist commanders "ripping off their masks" and switching sides in mid-battle. But there are also cases of the ex-tsarist commanders fighting valiantly.

An uneasy compromise is reached when Trotsky promotes the idea of appointing political commissars from the Party to keep watch on the military commanders. And the practice is so successful that Stalin will retain it when he comes to power. Only he will give it a Stalinesque twist of his own: during World War II, acting on Stalin's orders, the political commissars will issue all kinds of fantastic ultimatums, such as threatening to have military officers shot unless they take a given enemy position by sundown.

Such threats only serve to demoralize the soldiers, a fact to which Stalin is impervious, since he never really understands the military mind. He browbeats the army—they *could* do X, Y, and Z if only they wanted to—just as he browbeats the peasants, the workers, and even the scientists he recruits after World War II to create an atom bomb (the scientists finally complain that the coercion and house arrests only hinder their work). No command is ever impossible. No failure is ever the result of a natural cause. He has only one answer for those who cannot carry out his orders: "Shoot them! Shoot them all—traitors and saboteurs and lazy swine!"

THE YEAR 1919. The height of the Russian Civil War. A farm on the outskirts of Tsaritsyn. Young men between the ages of fifteen and twenty-five are tied to poles set a few feet apart. Their expressions range from defiance to abject misery as they await their execution. New recruits to the Red Army, they have been ambushed by royalist forces and brought to this command post, where they expect no mercy.

A flag fluttering over an abandoned farmhouse being used as a military headquarters, displays the double-headed eagle, the royal insignia. A White commander wearing the hated symbols of reaction, the epaulettes and medals abolished in the revolutionary army, struts in front of the condemned Reds.

"*Mes enfants, dety maee,*" he absurdly addresses them in both French and Russian in an affected, aristocratic drawl. "You have two choices. To cooperate and live. Or to refuse and die. Be assured, though, that we will get what we want from you before you die. Either way, the results will be the same for us."

He whispers with an aide, who stands respectfully at his side, before walking up and down among the prisoners, questioning them one by one. They either agree to his demand in a broken voice or scorn his offer. But when the farce is over, for a farce it turns out to be, the commander nods to his soldiers who shoot only those who have agreed to cooperate. Wild-eyed, the others stare as their bonds are loosened and they are embraced by their captors.

Soldiers come out of the farmhouse, dressed in the uniforms of Reds. The double-eagle is lowered while those soldiers who have been willing to die for the revolution are welcomed into the fold.

It takes them time to realize that they have been ambushed by their own brethren disguised as Whites, in a charade designed to test their loyalty. Yet they have passed the test and now can be trusted—those who do not suffer a nervous collapse, that is. They are congratulated by the commander with epaulettes and medals who has played the part of a White so well.

He is none other than Kamo, Stalin's former partner in bank robberies and extortions for the Party. He is particularly good, inspired, when playing a role. Before the revolution, while on a mission in Germany, he was caught red-handed; but he played the part of a madman so well, with so much wildness and realism, that he was locked up in an asylum, from which he escaped and returned to Russia.

But if Kamo is a good actor, Stalin writes the script. Stalin is the one forever trying to peer into men's souls, and into his own as well. For how else can he judge others but by the measure of his own treachery and violence and lust for power? Which means that even this elaborate charade has been in vain. The new "loyal" comrades, though they have been faithful unto death, can turn on him the next minute. The stratagem is not clever or effective but the evidence of an ailing mind. "I trust no one—not even myself," he is overheard to mutter one day, by visitors to his dacha. He is like the saint beset by demons in a medieval painting. Only he is himself a demon.

★   ★   ★

A SANITARIUM OUTSIDE MOSCOW, 1922. As Stalin walks down the gilded marble halls of what was once a grand-ducal palace, he hears a weird shrieking and babbling, sentences beginning with obscenities and ending in laughter and tears. Stalin's face is a mask of concentrated expectation as he ascends the grand staircase, enters a darkened bedroom, and approaches a huge canopied bed. He has come to visit the ailing Lenin who, though only a man in his fifties, is on his deathbed.

Stalin observes him calmly and leaves, now assured of the gravity of his condition. Although Lenin will rally, and even return to the Kremlin over the next months, it is only to be stricken a second time, and then a third, finally dying after a series of incapacitating strokes.

It is a stroke of good fortune for Stalin, against whom Lenin was preparing to move just before his illness. Since the end of the Civil War, the relationship between the two men has become more and more strained. It is a time of great exhaustion in Russia, following as it does the revolution, World War I, and the Civil War. But the Civil War has been won. The counterrevolutionaries have been pushed off Russian soil forever. And in the aftermath of war, as Lenin tries to construct the first Communist state, Trotsky and Stalin continue their battle, using a range of political and economic issues to express their mutual hatred. If Trotsky is the heir apparent, then Stalin is the would-be usurper.

It is during this time that Lenin's eyes begin to be opened: He is appalled by what he sees of Stalin's ruthlessness, his cynicism and vulgarity, his brutality toward his comrades. That Stalin has no concern for the welfare of the people would be excusable if it were in the name of some higher principle. But it becomes obvious to Lenin that Stalin is without principle, an intriguer, and that his supporters act like criminals and thugs.

An incident that occurs over the question of Georgia's national aspirations confirms Lenin's worst fears and suspicions. The question is a vital one for Lenin, who adamantly insists that Russian chauvinism not be allowed to run rampant. The revolution is a class struggle, workers against the capitalists, not a patriotic one of nation against nation. If former provinces of the tsarist empire such as Georgia, Finland, or the Ukraine want to break away, they have to be given that freedom, Lenin insists, a position Stalin mocks as naive. What is the point of giving away whole provinces to the bourgeoisie?

A former Georgian who now completely identifies with Great Russia, Stalin is particularly harsh when it comes to his native land. During a dispute in Georgia, one of his henchmen, Ordzhonikidze—later to be Stalin's minister of heavy industry, and still later to be killed by the Boss—brutally beats a Georgian Communist official who has the temerity to disagree with his, Ordzhonikidze's, and thus Stalin's, position. "Even in the days of the tsar, an official would not have been beaten in that way for respectfully differing with his superior," Lenin writes in a rage, ordering an investigation.

Stalin tries to placate Lenin by redrafting his plan for a Soviet constitution that would allow the various provinces to secede. But both men know it is a mere paper gesture that Stalin will make sure is circumvented in reality.

Lenin's first stroke intervenes. During his recovery he dictates his "political testament" to his faithful wife, Krupskaya, a woman who loathes Stalin and is in turned despised by him. Although the revolution preaches equality between the sexes, Stalin has a general dislike of intellec-

tual women (calling them "skinny herrings with ideas"),
and a particular hatred for Krupskaya. While he could tolerate a feminist such as Alexandra Kollontai, the author of
*The Autobiography of a Sexually Emancipated Communist
Woman* and the first female ambassador, there is a great difference between her and Krupskaya. Kollontai is a beautiful, charming woman, who delights in her femininity and
knows how to put such men as Stalin at their ease. Krupskaya is rather plain and stern, direct, earnest, suspicious,
and puritanical. It is Krupskaya who will see to it that her
husband's political testament is read publicly, to Stalin's dis-
comfiture, at a meeting of the Central Committee after
Lenin's death. It is a document Stalin tries to suppress, because it represents him in a negative light.

In the testament, Lenin evaluates the leaders of the
Party, warning that Stalin is too rude, too inconsiderate of
his comrades to be allowed to continue in a position of
power. "A way must be found to remove him," Lenin
writes—significant words. For Lenin finally realizes what
no one has seen up to this point: that Stalin has accumu-
lated a vast amount of power in the short time since the
end of the Civil War. He has worked silently, laboriously,
assuming the drudgery of organizational work that more
inspired Party members such as the orator-writer Trotsky
and the theorist-philosopher Bukharin avoided. But his
work in the new Soviet bureaucracy, especially in the In-
spectorate of Workers, has given Stalin a huge following;
countless Party chiefs from the provinces, from Moscow,
and from St. Petersburg owe him their jobs. Now he is no
longer a mere peasant factotum whom Lenin can remove
at will; but still, *a way must be found*.

The politburo, not yet apprised of Lenin's will and
worried about the health of the failing Father of the Revolution, appoints Stalin his "guardian." That is, it is Stalin's

job to make sure Lenin follows the doctors' orders, who have forbidden more than a few minutes a day of political correspondence and insist on rest and the avoidance of excitement.

In later years, Trotsky will accuse Stalin of poisoning Lenin, a charge for which there is no proof. Trotsky claims that an amoral man like Stalin would not shrink from stretching out his hand against the leader who he knew was planning to destroy him and whom he had at his mercy. The charge seems unlikely, not because Stalin would have had any scruples about killing Lenin, but simply because he did not have to. Lenin's condition was serious enough on its own. That Lenin asked Stalin for poison in case the condition became unbearable and that Stalin repeated this request to the politburo, might have further aroused suspicions in people's minds.

What Stalin did do, however, was attack Krupskaya as she was nursing her husband to his end, knowing that it would get back to Lenin. Distraught, Krupskaya wrote to a colleague asking him to intervene: "Lev Borisovich [Kamenev]! Yesterday Stalin subjected me to a storm of the coarsest abuse over a brief note that Vladimir Ilyich [Lenin] dictated to me with the permission of the doctors. I didn't join the Party yesterday. In the whole of these last thirty years, I have never heard a single coarse word from a comrade. The interests of the Party and of Ilyich are no less dear to me than to Stalin. At the moment I need all the self-control I can muster. I know better than all the doctors what can and what cannot be said to Ilyich, for I know what disturbs him and what does not, and in any case I know this better than Stalin.

"I am turning to you and to Gregory [Zinoviev] as much closer comrades of Vladimir Ilyich, and I beg you to protect me from gross interference with my private life and from vile abuse and threats. I have no doubt as to the unanimous decision of the Control Commission, with which Stalin takes it upon himself to threaten me. However, I have neither the time nor the energy to waste on such a stupid farce. I too am human and my nerves are at breaking point. N Krupskaya."

Knowing that Lenin needed absolute quiet and peace of mind—indeed, appointed by the politburo to ensure that no one bother the sick leader—did Stalin calculate that Lenin would hear of how he was treating his wife? Can there be any other explanation? Stalin's abuse of Krupskaya was repeated a second time, after which she went to Lenin in tears.

Lenin's letter to Stalin on this occasion miraculously survives. For some reason Stalin saved the damning reproach, which was found in his desk in the Kremlin after his death: "You allowed yourself to be so ill-mannered as to call my wife to the telephone and to abuse her," Lenin writes. "She has agreed to forget what was said. Nevertheless, she has told Zinoviev and Kamenev about it. I have no intention of forgetting what has been done against me, and it goes without saying that what was done against my wife, I also consider as having been directed against myself. I ask you, therefore, whether you are agreeable to withdrawing your words and apologizing or whether you prefer to break off relations between us."

Stalin apologizes, though in his note of apology he pretends not to understand what has aggrieved Lenin. Before the farce can go on any longer, however, Lenin dies. His body is embalmed and put on display despite his wishes for a small private funeral; Stalin understands the need of the Russian peasant for objects of veneration. The tomb becomes a place of pilgrimage—although there is some question whether the body is actually Lenin's. The

cadaver was damaged and had apparently started to de-
compose before the embalming process, which was not
entirely successful.

Months after Lenin's death, at Krupskaya's insistence,
his testament was read before a Central Committee meeting packed with Stalin's men. Zinoviev and Kamenev,
both of whom had worked hand in hand with Lenin on
the politburo, gave speeches in which they explained that
although Lenin feared Stalin would provoke divisions
among the politburo members, in fact there was only
peace and harmony among the members. Kamenev's
speech was even more emphatic than Zinoviev's, conclud-
ing that there was no reason to doubt Comrade Stalin. The
matter was passed over. But in the 1930s both Kamenev
and Zinoviev would be repaid for helping Stalin in his
hour of need. They were tortured mercilessly, forced to
sign false confessions, and executed. Zinoviev, a Jew, prayed
in Hebrew as he was dragged down the hall from his cell
to the execution block: *Shema Yisroel!* he shouted, "Hear,
O Israel! God is one!"

When one of the chiefs of Stalin's bodyguard, an ex-
barber and actor, began imitating Zinoviev and his prayers
and tears, Stalin laughed so hard that he had to hold his
stomach with one hand and motion for the man to stop
with the other. He wept with laughter.

Krupskaya, though, was another matter. She remained
a longtime critic of Stalin's, though by the '30s he prevented her from voicing her criticism in any public forum.
(During the purges she was wont to say that if Lenin were
alive, he would be executed.) She never forgot how Stalin
had conducted himself during Lenin's sickness and death,
and when Stalin's second wife killed herself, Krupskaya
took her revenge. Hearing that Stalin had allowed his wife
a religious burial—unheard of for a Party member—and

followed her coffin to the grave, and was generally beside himself with grief, she put a few lines in the newspaper by way of "consoling" him: "Dear Josef Vissarionych," it read, purposely misspelling Stalin's patronymic. "I have been thinking of you recently and wish to offer you my hand. It is hard to lose the person one is closest to. I remember some conversations I had with you in Ilyich's office during his illness. They gave me strength at the time. Again I press your hand. Nadezhda Krupskaya."

On the evening of February 26, 1939, Krupskaya invited her "friend" to celebrate her seventieth birthday. Stalin did not attend the party but he sent a cake. Later that evening, Krupskaya was stricken with severe food poisoning and rushed to a hospital. She died the following morning. At her funeral, Stalin carried the urn containing her ashes.

V.   WINNER TAKES ALL

The steps by which Stalin destroyed his enemies on the politburo and took supreme power are a history of shifting alliances, intraparty disputes, complicated maneuvers—pure Machiavelli. Trotsky being the forerunner, Stalin combines with Zinoviev and Kamenev, two powerful politburo members, against him. Once Trotsky is out of the way, Stalin combines with Bukharin to destroy Zinoviev and Kamenev, afterward moving against Bukharin as well. Suffice it to say, within five years all of his enemies are expelled from the Party and powerless. Trotsky is lucky to be sent into exile; his fame saves him, for a while. The others are tortured and executed, even though they "recant" and agree to say and do whatever Stalin wants of them.

Behind this wholesale destruction of Lenin's entire politburo, the most eminent figures of the Bolshevik old guard, it is possible to see a political goal. No one is left of any stature, reputation, or standing. Stalin cannot be challenged.

But the purges, which continue ad nauseam, have no practical results that benefit Stalin—just the opposite, they destroy some of Russia's best minds, some of the most loyal and dedicated Communists (not to mention almost the entire officer corps of the army). One old Bolshevik writes to Stalin to tell him that he first saw the light of day in the prison cell where his mother was serving a sentence for her dedication to the revolution. His every breath, his every action since then, has been taken in defense of the noble ideals of their party. Yet he has been beaten so badly that his spleen is ruptured; he has been degraded so brutally that he can barely think to write this letter. And by whom? By *teenagers,* just recruited to the Party and given absolute power over their victims. His letter goes unanswered.

Which is typical. Almost all appeals for mercy or justice fall on deaf ears. "A scoundrel and a male prostitute," Stalin will scrawl on a petition for mercy by an old comrade-in-arms, and when he sends the petition around to other politburo members, they invariably add "Exactly!" or "Shoot the mad dog!" knowing well that opposition would cost them their own lives.

If the terror may be said to have a point, it is its pointlessness. Anyone can be arrested and tortured at any time, including the torturers themselves. No one can feel secure. There is no such thing as innocence. There are instances of NKVD men breaking down and weeping during the interrogations: "Today it is you, tomorrow I am the one who will suffer. . . ."

The NKVD runs sanitariums to treat the nervous disorders of its thugs, the drunkenness and impotence endemic among its thousands of executioners and "interrogators," most of whom are in their late teens or early twenties. And it is no wonder; the degree of brutality practiced by the Bolsheviks either warps or drives crazy those charged with carrying out atrocities day after day. A general, the virtual ruler of a group of prisons containing more than a million souls, starts shrieking and hallucinating during an interrogation, yet he continues as commandant; his insanity does not incapacitate him in an insane system.

The purges are an endless series of accusations, made in the same hysterical mode as the Salem witch hunts. They take on the rhythm of a ritual of cleansing and sacrifice. "I can see from your eyes that you are a class enemy!" a woman shrieks during a local Party meeting, and that is enough; the person's life is over. (One quick-witted official thus accused shouts back, "And I can see from your eyes that you're a whore!" a comeback that saves his life and the lives of his family.)

The prisoners are made to confess, the prosecutor heaps abuse on them for their treachery, the crowds come to gawk, the newspapers are filled with the stories. And so life becomes "heroic," as it had been in the first days of the revolution. Spies and traitors are everywhere. The mindless horrific chaos continues at a heightened pitch.

The drama and sacrifice of revolutionary times captured the peoples' imagination and produced heroic results, but in the 1930s Stalin must find a way of turning the people to much more mundane tasks yet with the same ardor. There must be a second revolution for a weary nation. Enthusiasm has to be rekindled or there will be stagnation and disillusion. "You either burn or you rot."

Stalin is the earliest to propose a planned economy, and institutes his first five-year plan, meant to drag a backward Russia into the future posthaste. Fantastically high production quotas are set and the people are driven to meet them. Prize pickers of beets or miners who exceed their quotas are rewarded with medals and fame. Industrialization is equivalent to survival for Russia; after all, industrial nations rule the world. Stalin well understands that the wars of the future depend on the number of miles of railroad tracks, the amount of steel and iron produced. Though Stalin began his career by choosing "Koba" as his revolutionary name (in Georgian folklore, a robber-knight dedicated to the poor), the romance of heavy industry soon supplants the robber-knights in his imagination. It is the key to world power.

To be sure, agriculture plays its part in the grand scheme, too. In order to support industrial cities with huge populations of workers, agriculture must be more efficient, which means the small farms and plots of land have to be turned into collectives, where the harvesting can be done by machines. But the peasants are stubborn, attached to their land and unwilling to cooperate. Stalin sends thousands of Party workers to the country to "collect" food for the cities, by force, by murder and pillage. If the peasants will not give up their grain voluntarily, then he knows how to take it. And if there is not enough for both them and the cities, then they can starve.

When he is criticized by Party members, Stalin attacks the petit bourgeois intellectuals cut off from life, from the Party, from the workers and the revolution. For the rapid industrialization of the country, people are told to cut down on food, even on sex. "All our energies must be concentrated on heavy industry and production!" Stalin rants, and the nation listens.

Everywhere, the "rich" peasants, the kulaks (meaning "tight-fisted" in Russian) are put on trial, though their riches often consist of nothing more than a cow or a vegetable patch. Peasants set fire to their harvests and livestock rather than surrender them, and Stalin turns on them with redoubled fury. If they starve, so much the better—he will

teach them who rules Russia. The famine reaches staggering proportions. "They want to create a famine. They
slaughter the livestock. I will teach them what famine
means," Stalin threatens.

In the Ukraine alone, out of twenty million peasants,
five million will die. Guards will take away their wheat,
their grain will be left to blacken on the stalk. Stalin will
never forgive.

His soldiers arrive in a village and announce: "We have
been commandeered here and have been charged to help
you to fulfill the quota of grain procurements. There is a
deficiency of a hundred million poods in grain deliveries?
What does that mean? Hunger, widespread starvation in
the cities, in industrial centers, in the Red Army. You say
the plan for procurements cannot be fulfilled? Nonsense—
there is plenty of grain. The kulaks' barns and sheds are
overflowing. *Every* kulak's household has fifty thousand or
sixty thousand poods he has not given to the state. The kulaks want the state to double or triple prices before they
sell the staff of life. There is a law to deal with that: article
107 of the Penal Code: against speculation, against buying
or hoarding."

Students are taken from universities and sent out into
the country to help bring back whatever grain is to be
found. Photographs from the period show the skeletons of
the aged and the young who have lain down by the road-
side to die. And still patriotic speeches are made to the
dying: "Give up your wheat for the Fatherland!"

Olga Alliluyeva, Stalin's mother-in-law and onetime
mistress, was a woman from the country. She urges her
daughter to plead for the peasants. With scorn, Stalin turns
on his wife, Nadezhda, now herself the mother of two
young children, and mocks her. For good measure he adds,
"Who are you? What are you? You're either mine or

Kurnatevsky's!" meaning that she, his wife, is either his own daughter or the daughter of Kurnatevsky, another revolutionary who had made love to her mother at the same time he had.

Surely, this doubt must have preyed on the young woman, already severely depressed by the prisonlike atmosphere of the Kremlin, inhabited by much older people obsessed with ambition and power, with guards listening and watching in every corner. Then, too, Stalin would be withdrawn for days, hardly speaking to his family. Or he would turn the full force of his sarcasm and brutality on them. His son will later drink himself to death while his daughter will lead an unhappy life, first defecting from and then returning to the USSR, torn between Russia and the West.

At a banquet held at War Commissar Voroshilov's, Stalin pushes his wife beyond her endurance. "Hey you!" he drunkenly calls to her. She arises in a rage. "I'm not 'Hey you!' to anyone!" she shouts. He showers her with obscenities and she leaves the banquet weeping. Paulina Molotov walks around the Kremlin grounds for hours with her, listening to her complaints and finally seeing her to her room. The next morning a brief announcement shocks the world: the young Nadezhda Alliluyeva Stalina is dead. The children are sent to Stalin's dacha in the country. Stalin reads and rereads the suicide note she left before shooting herself. It is filled with accusations, and reproaches him for his crimes. He follows her coffin to the Novodivichy Cemetery, where he sits by her grave sunk in thought. Then he returns to the Kremlin and drinks himself into a stupor. Truly she was her mother's daughter, temperamental and fiery. But was she her father's too?

VI. THE GREAT CRISIS

When it came to Hitler, Stalin was like a rabbit paralyzed in front of a boa constrictor.
—Nikita Khrushchev

JUNE 22, 1941, Moscow. Stalin is awakened in the middle of the night and told that German troops have smashed through the border defenses and are rapidly advancing through hundreds of miles of Russian territory. The Russian positions are falling one by one, Russian planes are being destroyed on the ground, Russian soldiers are being taken prisoner by the thousands. It is a disaster of the first magnitude.

For a long time he remains silent, breathing heavily into the phone as if gasping for breath. Then he whispers in a broken voice that the members of the politburo must come to the Kremlin. He knows that it is his responsibility, that he has ignored the many warnings that poured in from foreign and Russian sources alike. The massing of German troops on the Russian border, the daily violations of Russian airspace—he has shrugged off every sign, forbidding the Russian troops to go on alert or prepare for war, so as not to provoke Hitler.

Right up until the moment of the attack, he fulfills his pact with Hitler, insisting that strategic war material be delivered exactly on time. How could a man so watchful, so mistrustful and paranoid, make such a mistake? The truth of the matter is that the same paranoia that permits him to kill millions with psychopathic ease clouds his vision here. His paranoia is turned on the Western democracies, on England, France, and America: surely *they* are behind all the reports, which are mere disinformation, intended to disrupt the relationship between Nazi Germany and Communist Russia. His reasoning runs something like this: war between Russia and Germany would take the pressure off the democracies and lead to the destruction of communism. The Western democracies want to sic Hitler on Russia. They want to see a communist state destroyed at any price because it threatens their existence by providing an example to their workers.

For the first week of the war, Stalin is nowhere to be seen, nowhere to be heard. He has Molotov address the nation while he himself retires to his dacha near Moscow in a state of collapse. The Committee for National Salvation is formed without his being present—unheard of, unthinkable. And when a delegation finally does arrive from the Kremlin to seek his advice and guidance, he actually expects that they have come to arrest him.

But the habit of blind obedience, and the fear of the tyrant, is so ingrained that no one suggests rebellion. He has destroyed thousands of potential opponents, and those who have survived understand that their survival is conditional upon absolute acceptance of Stalin as a demigod. If he has delivered the nation into Hitler's hands by refusing to mobilize, refusing to allow the most elementary steps in self-defense, then it *must be so.*

Stalin finally pulls himself together, returns to the

Kremlin, and addresses the nation, reminding the people of their heroic past. *Brothers! Sisters!* They will repel the foreign invader from Russia's soil now, just as Kutuzov threw back Napoleon. It is shocking to hear the name of a tsarist general on his lips; but from this moment on Stalin has one concern: to win the war, by any means. If the past can be used to boost morale, then ideology becomes insignificant. Generals and scientists and priests are liberated from prison camps to help in the defense. English and American diplomats are welcomed in the Kremlin. By the time the Germans have reached Stalingrad, three and a-half million Russian soldiers have been taken prisoner and two million are dead.

"Lenin left us a state and we made shit out of it," Stalin says at a politburo meeting. The Germans are at the gates of Moscow. The main government offices are evacuated; the city is put under military rule. But Stalin himself decides to remain.

It is a momentous decision, which prevents panic. Having thrown himself into the war, Stalin never falters thereafter. He directs the war with a firm hand. He has destroyed the morale of the army by executing its best officers during the purges, yet he is sure of the soldiers' loyalty. Their obedience is so absolute that Stalin can even, on occasion, yield to their judgment at critical moments without fear. Marshal Zhukov, the liberator of Moscow, will be permitted to speak to the Boss roughly, honestly—although after the war he will be relegated to a remote post as Stalin claims all the glory for himself.

Stalin works night and day, aging twenty years. Those who see him after the war are shocked at his appearance. But Russia is saved. At what price, no one will ever really know. The actual figures are kept secret out of fear. Some estimates run as high as twenty million Russians dead.

At the victory parade after the war, the Nazi standards and flags are thrown at Stalin's feet. As he accepts the homage, though, literally thousands of bodyguards accompany his every move. He has conquered the enemy without, but not the one within.

VII. THE OLD ORACLE

Today the mice have buried the cat.
> —Khrushchev, at Stalin's funeral

FEBRUARY, 1953, a modest dacha in the countryside outside Moscow. The shutters are closed and the drapes are drawn. An old man sits alone at a table piled high with books the censor has forbidden; with papers marked "Urgent"; with the pale blue folders NKVD chief Beria uses for reports on the men and women in prison camps; and with the dark red folders used for reports on the nuclear weapons program, a project of which Beria is also in charge—despite the fact that it is widely known that he is given to abducting very young girls, kidnapping them off the street and driving them back to his palatial home, where he drugs and rapes them.

But he understands the Boss and that's what counts: he has written a history of the revolution in Georgia that praises his fellow Georgian Stalin to the skies, and his secret reports now cleverly play on Stalin's suspicions and fears. There are detailed accounts of the doings of artists, writers, and generals—even General Zhukov, especially Zhukov, the hero of World War II, defender of Moscow and taker of Berlin, because to rival Stalin's fame is to court danger. There are files on relatives of Stalin's first and second wives, thick dossiers on Stalin's most important officials, the commissar of foreign affairs, the commissar of war, of heavy industry; and a mountain of paper on the wives and children of these colleagues, the results of intensive spying.

But all of these urgent memos and special reports, including one regarding a breakthrough in Soviet nuclear capability, have been pushed aside. Instead, the old man sits cutting pictures from magazines, idealized photos of small children, to be pasted up on the bare walls; a little girl feeding a lamb, a little boy picking flowers near a river.

Could this really be the man known to the world as the man of steel? If one knew the "Leader of the Workers of the World" only from his glamorous posters or larger-than-life statues, it would be impossible to recognize him in the muttering old man hunched over the table. In repose, his eyes are yellow and unfocused and his expression is vacant. But in an instant his features can become contorted with insane rage, or darkened with suspicion, or lit up with sardonic, sadistic laughter. His breath is foul, because his teeth, neglected for decades, are rotting and abscessed.

But to urge Stalin to see a dentist is to risk becoming an object of his suspicions, those close to him know. He will immediately think it is part of a plot to kill him while he is being treated. His closest associates, Malenkov, Beria, Khrushchev, & Co. finally try to bring up the subject, but they do so gingerly, in a roundabout way: they praise the fine teeth of one of his cooks, a man they coach to smile when he brings a favorite dish to the table. The plan backfires, though, because when Stalin feels depressed he hates to see anyone in a good mood. The cook is subjected to a barrage of abuse but considers himself lucky to escape with his life.

And he *is* lucky, given the arbitrary nature of the arrests and executions in Stalin's last years. Men are murdered, sometimes together with their entire families, for reasons as absurd as the cook's grin. Or for failing to meet Stalin's gaze frankly or for meeting it *too* frankly!—there is no telling how one should act. Since the purges began, it is no longer possible to discern the reasons for torture and execution. This is the nature of absolute power as exercised by Stalin. It is godlike and inexplicable.

For the two hundred million people under his power, his fantasy becomes reality. If he wishes for a person or even for an entire ethnic group to be guilty they are guilty. Tens of thousands of Tatars, the young and the old, men, women, and children, are deported in packed cattle cars to a barren place of exile. They arrive weakened from hunger and thirst. The train, without windows or bathrooms, has stopped periodically for those who have died on the way to be thrown into mass graves dug by relatives at gunpoint.

The Jews are also on Stalin's list. Just before he dies, he is planning a mass deportation of all European Jews to the edge of the Gobi desert, a measure supported by Kaganovich, a ruthless member of the inner circle who is eager to prove that he is "a Communist, not a Jew." Half the doctors at the Kremlin hospital are put on trial because they are Jewish. The doctors are accused of trying to murder Stalin, but are saved by his death. Later, Khrushchev will release them from prison, stating publicly that there was no basis for the "doctors' plot" and even putting on trial the NKVD lackeys who produced the false evidence.

Stalin's anti-Semitism is a lifelong prejudice, but it does not become obsessive until the last phase of his life, when he becomes paranoid about a Jewish threat. A surprisingly large number of important Party figures during the revolution were Jews (Kamenev, Zinoviev, Kaganovich, Litvinov, to name a few). This led Stalin to "notice" that a disproportionate number of senior government officials in the politburo were married to Jews. Foreign Minister Molotov, Minister of Culture Zhdanov, War Minister Voroshilov, etc., all had Jewish wives, not to mention the fact that both Stalin's son and his daughter had married Jews. His paranoia triggered, Stalin decides in 1953 that all this has been part of a Zionist-American plot, even though the Soviet Union had originally supported the young socialist state of Israel in 1948; Golda Meir was the first Israeli ambassador to Moscow. However, even earlier, before his paranoia focused so intensely on the Zionists, there were signs of what was to come: Paulina Molotov was seen talking in Hebrew to Ambassador Meir in 1948 and was packed off for five years to isolation in a prison camp.

Before each politburo meeting in the early '50s, Foreign Minister Molotov asks Beria about his wife. "How is Paulina?" he whispers before Stalin arrives, and Beria whispers back, "Still alive!" Molotov's silence in Stalin's presence is typical of the servility that surrounds the old dictator. Sycophants vie with each other in inventing praise. Not only is Stalin all-knowing, all-seeing, the genius-leader of the world's workers, but it is proposed—and unanimously approved at a Party Congress—that "the calendar should start with the birth of Stalin, not with the birth of Christ." (Stalin declines the honor.) The head of the Writers' Union declares that when he has a son, the first word he will teach him to say will be "Stalin." And Kaganovich slyly protests at a meeting of the inner circle that while he has never known Stalin to make a mistake, he must point out an error the leader has fallen into. There is breathless silence. Astonished stares. "Yes," Kaganovich smoothly continues, "Stalin *undervalues* his own importance and tends to exalt that of Lenin. It should be the other way around."

The inner circle is on continuous call, since in his last years Stalin often gets lonely. Khrushchev describes drunken dinners complete with coarse jokes and childish games that go on until dawn. These are usually preceded by hours in the Kremlin movie theater. "Stalin used to select the movies himself," Khrushchev writes. ". . . He liked American cowboy movies especially. He used to curse them and give them the proper ideological evaluation, but then immediately order new ones. The films didn't have subtitles, so Bolshakov [the minister of cinematography] would translate them out loud. He would translate from all languages. Actually, he didn't know any of these languages. He had been told the plot in advance. He would take pains to memorize it and then would 'translate' the movie. . . . We often joked about his translations. Beria especially. In many of the scenes, Bolshakov would simply get the plot wrong, or else he would just explain what anyone could see was happening on the screen: 'Now he's leaving the room. Now he's walking across the street.' Beria would then chime in and give Bolshakov some help: 'Look! He's started running! Now he's running!'"

Such are the vagaries of the old man, terrible and unpredictable. For the last week the business of government has ground to a halt because he has not felt like working. Everything depends on him, everything requires his approval, from a contract with a foreign company for spare tractor parts to the decision to execute a ten-year-old boy accused of being a spy—an absurd horror typical of Stalin's Russia. He has created for himself a staggering and all-consuming responsibility, which has aged and wasted him. But after thirty years of power, "the genius-leader of the world's workers" has periods during which the strain of a lifetime of intense labor and unhealthy habits tells. He forgets the names of his closest associates, or turns his attention from a pressing matter such as the Korean war to writing a long essay on linguistics for *Pravda,* though his knowledge of the subject is rudimentary.

But whatever distractions he turns to, linguistics or biology, supporting the theories of Lysenko, a crank scientist who falsifies the results of his experiments; or clipping photos from magazines; or endlessly sketching wolves on an oversize pad, always the same picture, obsessively drawn again and again, he is never free from his lifelong mania: conspiracy.

If age has diminished his capacity for work, it has intensified his fears and morbid suspicions. As the old man sits doodling, guards circle the high walls of the dacha without pause, on skis in winter, on bicycles in summer, circle within concentric circle of soldiers in perpetual motion, like flies hovering around a sugar bowl. Within the walls is another set of walls, with attack dogs and machine-gun toting guards in between and NKVD spies watching the guards.

It is a nation of spies, spies spying on spies in an infinitely receding hall of mirrors. Soldiers denounce their officers, workers eavesdrop on their bosses, children betray their parents and are rewarded with medals and pathetic adulation in the propaganda press. "My father is nothing more than a class enemy to me!" an eleven-year-old boy says after hearing his father complain about the long work hours on the collective farm. Is he indifferent to his father's fate, which is to be brutally beaten and worked to death in the Siberian gold mines, or is it that he does not fully understand it? The Komsomol, the Communist youth cadres, are dedicated to forging bonds between its members that are stronger than any other.

Only Death can bypass all the guards and walls and sophisticated screening systems. Stalin collapses late at night when he is alone in his dacha. Khrushchev, Beria, Molotov, and the other members of the inner circle are summoned by guards, who are concerned because the Boss has gone for hours without calling for food or drink as he usually does at night. They enter the room and find him on the floor. Shrugging his condition off as drunkenness, they have him placed on his bed to sleep it off. Hours later they are summoned again: Stalin's sleep is unnatural. His housekeeper is worried. Finally, after more than twelve hours of delay, medical attention is summoned. His comrades obviously have much to gain by their master's death and nothing to gain from his recovery.★

A vigil begins, which is truly nightmarish as described by his daughter and by Khrushchev. Khrushchev writes, "As soon as Stalin showed signs of consciousness Beria threw himself on his knees, seized Stalin's hand and started kissing it. When Stalin lost consciousness again and closed his eyes, Beria stood up and spat . . . spewing hatred. It was unbearable to listen to him."

Moving in and out of consciousness, Stalin points to one of the pictures overhead, of the lamb being fed by a

---

★On the Jewish holiday of Purim in 1953, the Lubavitcher Rebbe, leader of a Chasidic group that fled Russia during WWII, publicly prayed for Stalin's destruction. At the same time that the Rebbe, together with thousands of his followers, chant, *"Hu ra! He is evil!"* Stalin suffers the stroke that will finish him. The record of the Rebbe's public talks, the *"Sichos"* for 1953, attest to the fact: Stalin left the world accompanied by Jewish curses and prayers for deliverance.

little girl. Those present say it was as if he was saying that he, the great Stalin, was now as helpless as that lamb.

"The death agony was terrible," his daughter, Svetlana, will record. "God grants an easy death only to the just. He literally choked to death as we watched. At what seemed like the very last moment he suddenly opened his eyes and cast a glance over everyone in the room. It was a terrible glance, insane or maybe angry, and full of the fear of death. . . . Then something incomprehensible happened that to this day I can't forget. He suddenly lifted his left hand, as though he were pointing to something up above and bringing down a curse on us all. The gesture was full of menace. The next moment he was dead."

A visitor to Stalin's dacha once found him playing with his young daughter, whom he called "his little housekeeper" after his wife's suicide, a job the child took very seriously. On this occasion, she was reproaching her father for something and he was pleading for mercy.

"No, no, don't tell cook!" he whined with mock terror. "It will be all over with me if you do!"

"I don't care. You have been bad and you will be punished!" she said sternly, at which he burst into a shout of laughter.

Is it possible to imagine the motives, the pleasures, the hatreds of such a man? When he was alone, did he himself know who he was?

SADDAM
HUSSEIN

I. THE POWER OF HATRED

I was awake all night—hating.
　　—Bismarck

NOVEMBER 1988, a mansion on an island in the Tigris called Umm al-Khanazir, The Mother of Pigs. A big bash is in progress whose guests include high officials and army officers, oil entrepreneurs, diplomats, and a special foreign guest, Suzanne Mubarak, the wife of the Egyptian president. A singer croons a well-known Iraqi song, "Saddam, O Saddam, You Great and Powerful One," as waiters circulate with choice food catered from Maxime's and flown in from Paris that day. It is to be a fateful party, one that will start a cycle of family violence and rage.

The host is Saddam Hussein's close friend and pimp, Kamel Hannah, who is giving the banquet as a state event at the request of the president, who is not in attendance.

A low hedge separates the mansion from another palatial building next to it where a second party is in progress. This one is being given by Uday Hussein, Saddam Hussein's son, a vicious and arrogant young man who has vowed that he will be more cruel than his father when he takes power. If Uday sees a woman he wants, he tears her from her boyfriend or husband, shooting the man if he protests. One of his victims, an army officer and war hero, was murdered in this way in a Baghdad disco only a few nights earlier.

Uday's party is meant to annoy Kamel Hannah, who has snubbed him. The two became enemies when Uday's mother, Sajida, began complaining bitterly about Kamel Hannah and his women. Above all, she blames Hannah for having introduced her husband to a sexy young ophthalmologist, Samira al-Shahbander. Tired of ambitious women, Hussein had immediately been intrigued by the spirited young Samira, who was cool and played hard to get. The dictator courted her with lavish gifts and extravagant gestures for many months before she finally relented.

As their relationship deepened, the affair became more than a diversion. Samira divorced her husband and secretly became Saddam's second wife—Muslims can have four—finally moving into a wing of the presidential palace when she became pregnant.

This insult to Saddam's first wife will split the family. Sajida moves to a villa on the presidential grounds and stirs up her son Uday against her now mortal enemy Kamel Hannah, harping on the disgrace she has suffered because of his pimping. Nothing comforts her, not her jewels, which are legendary, not her million-dollar shopping sprees in Europe at the most exclusive fashion houses, not her villa filled with priceless antiques and works of art. Endlessly, she repeats the refrain: her father took Saddam Hussein in when he was a dirt-poor village boy; she and he were betrothed as children; now he has married one of his "whores."

All of which is in the air on the night of the two parties. Uday's guests include underworld figures and prostitutes and decadent young hangers-on who cater to his every whim, as does his bodyguard-double, Latif Yahia, who loathes Uday and who later defects, becoming a source of valuable firsthand information. On the other side of the hedge are Kamel Hannah's guests, statesmen and generals and businessmen, who lounge near the pool amidst lush flowers or dance in the plush gold rooms of the mansion.

As the evening wears on, Kamel Hannah, tipsy and happy, dances on a table and fires "joy shots" in the air. Uday sends someone to tell him to stop and receives the reply, "Kamel Hannah takes orders only from the president."

In a rage, Uday starts across the hedge, picking up a battery-powered electric knife called the Magic Wand, an instrument used to cut roses. Stalking through rooms filled with elegant guests, he finds Kamel Hannah still dancing on a table in the main banquet hall. "Get down!" he shouts, and his father's adviser jumps down to face him.

"I told you to be quiet," Uday snarls.

"I only listen to your father, the president," Hannah repeats, and the next moment Uday strikes him across his head with the Wand, opening an ugly gaping wound. Hannah staggers back in shock as Uday slashes his throat. Women shriek, and Mme. Mubarak's bodyguards surround her as the mortally wounded pimp falls to the ground. Kamel Hannah's brother, an intelligence officer, tries to run forward to kill Uday but Uday's bodyguards restrain him. Kamel Hannah, dying, reaches for his gun to shoot Uday but Uday kicks it away and pumps half a dozen bullets from his own gun into Hannah before walking through the now silent crowd, through the hedge, and back to his own party. Amidst the ensuing chaos, an army officer telephones the president.

★　　★　　★

A Mercedes accompanied by military vehicles races through the streets of Baghdad. It screeches to a stop at the entrance of the Ibn-Sina Hospital, where two ambulances arrived earlier that night. The door of the car is thrown open and a disheveled Saddam Hussein jumps out, his eyes filled with rage. Moving like a lion, he strides into a room where doctors are desperately trying to revive a dead man. For a long moment, Hussein stands staring at his close friend. Clenching his fists, he rushes down the hall and into another room, where doctors have begun to pump the stomach of the twenty-four-year-old Uday, who has taken an overdose of pills—or so he says—in fear of his father's wrath.

Pushing the doctors aside, Hussein slaps his son's face again and again. "Your blood will flow like my friend's!" he shouts, smashing a glass partition and leaving the terrified doctors to continue their work. He speeds back through the night to Project 2000, the $500 million palace built for him by European architects and designers. And here, amidst almost barbaric splendor, he gives vent to his rage, ordering his lackeys to set fire to his son's fleet of more than a hundred luxury cars in all models and colors, Jaguars, Ferraris, Maseratis, Porsches, Mercedeses. His first-born has killed his pimp, and this is just the beginning, he vows: he will make the "lion cub" suffer.

In terror, Sajida phones Jordan's King Hussein, crying hysterically that her husband is going to murder her son. The Jordanian king immediately flies to Iraq to help mediate in the family dispute; he succeeds in cooling Saddam's anger toward his son.

The brawl is instructive, revealing as it does the primitive nature of Hussein and his family. And this one word, "family"—clan, tribe—is the key to how Saddam Hussein achieved power and how he holds on to it. The security police, all the chief ministries are controlled by men related to one or another of Hussein's two family clans, the al-Majids, his father's cousins, and the Ibrahims, his half-brothers, sons from his mother's second marriage.

Which is why this chasm opening up in the family is dangerous. Every day Saddam's brother-in-law, the minister of war, Adnan Khairallah Tulfah, comes to visit his sister Sajida in a show of support for the wronged wife. Similarly, Khairallah Tulfah, Saddam's father-in-law, had been Saddam's mentor and was for a time mayor of Baghdad after his protégé took power. An important clan member, the old man is now bitter about Saddam's treatment of his daughter.

And so it goes, with various family factions taking sides. Saddam sends his son abroad to his half-brother in Switzerland, who handles his foreign investments and is Iraq's ambassador to the UN at The Hague. Uday will be charged there with carrying a concealed weapon and returned to Iraq, but for now the president has breathing space, a chance to mend family fences and quiet the scandal at home, with the murdered man's family, ironically, pleading for mercy for Uday in the newspapers.

The quarrel touches Hussein in a way that international political or economic pressure cannot. There is nothing else to hold on to but family in Hussein's world, no one else to trust. An old Arab saying, "Myself and my cousin against the world," reflects this feeling of blood ties being the one reliable bond in a world of shifting allegiances and treachery. The feeling is deeply rooted in the history of Iraq, which up until World War I was not a nation at all but merely three backward provinces of the Ottoman Empire. The corrupt Turkish officials were mainly interested in leeching as much money as they could from the subject Kurds and Arabs who lived under their rule. And so, during the five hundred years of Ottoman rule, a man or a woman looked to the tribe for protection and justice and a sense of identity. Yet the individual was isolated amidst tribal blood feuds and intense hatred over religious differences, Muslim against Muslim, the schismatic Shiites against the orthodox Sunnis. In the face of danger, kinsmen were everything.

The world into which Saddam Hussein is born in 1937 has not changed much for generations, though after World War I, control has passed from the Ottomans, to the British, to a British-backed monarchy in 1921. Britain gives up its mandate after a series of bloody rebellions prove too costly, yet it maintains control indirectly. A son of the Hashemite family of Mecca is elevated to the throne with the understanding that the source of his power is in the West. The king, Faisal I, an astute and honorable man, might try to mediate between his subjects and his British backers, but the brutal truth of the matter is that his country's resources are controlled by a small oligarchy and are used in service to the West. Discontent finds expression in unsuccessful coups and occasional massacres. Hundreds of Assyrians, an ancient Christian people, are mutilated and slaughtered by a frenzied crowd, which parades the dismembered bodies. Similarly, the centuries-old Jewish quarter of Baghdad is attacked, its inhabitants murdered and hate-filled messages scrawled with their blood on the city walls. However, these blood baths change nothing. Despite its independence, Iraq remains asleep, sunk in the feudalism and ignorance of the past.

Nowhere can this be seen more clearly than in the little village of al-Ouja, about a hundred miles north of Baghdad, where Saddam Hussein is born. It is nothing but a cluster of baked-mud houses, no running water, no electricity, no paved streets, no opportunity for anything but a crushing life of poverty and petty thievery. Indeed, the child's very survival is something like a miracle, given the high rate of infant mortality in Iraq.

Hussein's father dies before he is born, and his mother, Subha, a poor and illiterate peasant woman, soon marries another man, Ibrahim al-Hassan, a thief known as "The Liar." The Liar finds the child a nuisance, so Subha sends Saddam, no older than two or three, to live with his uncle, his father's brother, in the nearby town of Takrit.

Takrit, like al-Ouja, is also a place of mud houses and dusty, unpaved streets and poverty. Still, it is larger, it is on the Baghdad-Mosul railroad line, and it has inspiring historical connections: fierce Arab fighters have inhabited its fortress, now in ruins, and the great Arab conqueror, Suleiman the Magnificent, acknowledged it as his birthplace eight hundred years before. Saddam's uncle Khairallah Tulfah has a young daughter the same age as the boy, and a marriage is arranged between the children which will take place when they are grown. The small girl collecting cow dung to use for fuel will one day be the bejeweled Sajida pouting in the president's guest villa over her husband's infidelity.

Saddam's uncle Khairallah, an officer in the Royal Iraqi Army, is an ardent Arab nationalist who despises the monarchy both for its pro-Western stance and its narrow Iraqi interests. He will pass on his passion for politics to Saddam, who drinks in the heated debate in his uncle's house from his earliest years. Khairallah is with those who want a unified Arab nation stretching from the fertile crescent to the Nile, a modern, secular state strong enough to defy the West. But this is a dream, an unrealizable ideal. The real question of the day is how Iraq can throw off the British yoke, since there is no doubt that Great Britain is the power behind the throne. Throughout the 1930s, Iraq remains what it was at its creation: an artificial state with no emotional core, no national identity.

King Faisal I dies in 1933 at the age of fifty-six, lamenting this fact. "With a heart full of sorrow, I say there is still no Iraqi people," he remarks in a speech just before his death, "but only unimaginable masses of human beings devoid of any patriotic ideas, imbued with religious traditions and absurdities, connected by no common tie, giving ear to evil, prone to anarchy and perpetually ready to rise against any government whatsoever."

Faisal's playboy son, Ghazi, takes his place, but after a few frantic years of pleasure, Ghazi dies in 1939 when he smashes his sports car into a pole when drunk. Which leaves the five-year-old Faisal II as king, with a pro-British regent and a wily pro-British prime minister, Nuri al-Said—who will have been appointed prime minister fourteen times by the end of his long career. The year 1941 seems to be Iraq's; Britain's resources are strained to the limit, and the new prime minister, Rashid Ali, is pro-Nazi. Ali attempts to overthrow the monarchy, hoping for help from the Germans, and Saddam's uncle Khairallah is among those army officers who join in the coup.

But Hitler is too busy in Russia to send help. The rebels are left high and dry, and after a short interval the British send troops from India and restore the child-monarch and his regent and prime minister. Rashid Ali is executed together with many of the rebels, while others, Saddam's uncle among them, are sentenced to prison. Thus Saddam Hussein, barely five years old at the time, is sent back from his uncle's house in Takrit to his mother in al-Ouja, where the Liar, his stepfather, humiliates and beats the boy every chance he gets. Swinging an asphalt-covered stick, he makes Saddam dance to avoid its blows, just as years later Saddam will make his victims dance on the corpses of their relatives. Lazy and cruel, the Liar uses the boy to steal sheep from the neighboring farms, awakening him every morning by pulling his hair brutally and shouting, "Get up, son of a whore!"

Five years pass in this way, during which Saddam learns to hate. At the age of ten he rejoices: his uncle is released from prison. Saddam wishes to rejoin him and learn to read and write like his cousin, Khairallah's son Adnan. But this time the Liar objects to the boy's being sent away: he is useful as a servant and a thief. Saddam's seven-year-old cousin, Adnan, convinces him to defy the Liar and leave for Takrit. It is a heroic step for the young Saddam, who is set on having whatever "the large world," Takrit, has to offer.

Because of his treason, his uncle has been forced to resign from the army and now works as a schoolteacher. But the violence of his political opinions has only increased. Khairallah publishes a vile pamphlet, *Three Whom God Should Not Have Created: Jews, Persians and Flies,* which Saddam listens to with awe. His uncle's political hatred is now added to the seething cauldron of the young boy's intense emotions.

Thus it is that in 1947 a boy in ragged clothes is seen hiding in the ruined fortress overlooking Takrit. He crouches beneath its crumbling gates or slinks in the shadow of its ancient walls to get away from the other boys, who taunt him. He is ten years old but he cannot read. He comes from a smaller, poorer town which they despise. The teacher's questions have revealed his background.

"Fatherless one!" they shout at the outsider, chasing him through the ruins. "Be damned!"

Younger than they but more cunning, the boy escapes. In a back alley near his uncle's house, he grabs up an iron bar which he then uses to revenge himself, waylaying his tormentors one by one and beating them into submission.

It is fitting that the boy is called Saddam, for the name means "confrontation" or "holding fast" in Arabic. And he *will* hold fast, both as boy and as man, defying the world in one battle after another for the rest of his life.

II. REVOLUTION, IRAQI STYLE

BAGHDAD, THE 1950s. Together with his nephew, Saddam, his son, Adnan, and his daughter, Sajida, Khairallah has moved to a poor section of Baghdad, al Karkh, where others from Takrit are living, peasants and ex-officers and merchants who could not make a living at home. The Takritis, a closely knit and like-minded group, extort and thieve, using Mafia tactics, in between drinking sweet tea and arguing politics.

During this decade, the teenage Saddam will learn the ins and outs of Iraqi politics not only from Khairallah, but from a host of friends and family members, officers and ex-officers in the Iraqi army, which has grown enormously in size and influence since the death of Faisal I. The army is the main venue for political power and will only become more significant as a player.

Saddam's school grades are too poor for him to enter the military academy. It is a failure that humiliates and haunts him, surrounded as he is by members of his clan who have risen in the ranks. When he finally assumes power, he will shower himself with every military honor available, designating himself marshal and sporting endless uniforms and medals, like a starving man falling on a feast. More significant, though, is the effect that this exclusion from the military will have during the Iraq-Iran wars. His megalomania, fueled by his inferiority complex, will bring on disaster and cause the death of tens of thousands of his soldiers when this self-proclaimed "marshal" ignores his generals' strategic advice.

Despite Saddam's exclusion from the academy, some of his military relatives will take him under their wing. A figure who will be especially important in this respect is an older cousin, Ahmed Hassan al-Bakr, a brigadier who will later advance Saddam *precisely because* he failed to enter the academy, making him an outsider among the ambitious army officers and thus no threat to his cousin. (As a result, the young dictator will acquire a perfect reputation: he will be perceived as being both brutal and backward, a useful yet controllable ally in the violent world of Iraqi politics.)

Iraq is in a ferment as Saddam comes to maturity. The rising star of the Arab world is the Egyptian president, Nasser. It is impossible to ignore the example of Nasser who has just transformed Egypt. The charismatic leader is either loved, or feared and hated. With the Egyptian revolution in 1952, Nasser and his fellow army officers have ousted the pleasure-loving and weak King Farouk, who is a mirror image of the weak Iraqi monarch, Faisal II. Boldly, Nasser nationalizes the Suez Canal and calls on the Arabs to unite (for a time he will actually succeed in forging a union between Egypt and Syria and Yemen, the short-lived United Arab Republic). The pro-Western Arab monarchies are blamed for the Arab humiliation at the hands of the young state of Israel, and though the monarchy holds on to power in Iraq, its days are numbered.

Pan-Arab ideals are in the air, in one form or another.

In the 1920s a Syrian Christian and a Sunni Arab from Damascus found the Baath Party. Taking its name from the Arabic word for rebirth or resurrection, the Baath Party draws its support from men like Saddam's uncle Khairallah who feel shame at Arab weakness in the face of Western imperialism. At this time, the Iraqi wing of the Baath has a coterie of no more than three hundred members, who preach that the Arabs are a single people destined to form one great nation. The teenage Saddam is recruited by the Baathists to organize demonstrations for the small movement.

The confused philosophy of the Baath Party combines many disparate and contradictory elements: mystical nationalism of the nineteenth-century German sort; a loose, unscientific socialism; a call to throw off traditional Muslim shackles; an appreciation of Arab culture, poetry, and music; and even a secular appreciation of the Koran for having inspired Arabs to empire centuries before. More important to Saddam than its philosophy, however, is the fact that many of his clan members and friends from Takrit are prominent in the fledgling Iraqi branch of the Baathists.

It is not the Baath Party, however, which overthrows the Iraqi monarchy in 1958, but a shrill-voiced, ascetic, and idealistic general, Abdul Karim Qassim, who rebels when he is sent to support the pro-French regime of Camille Chamoun in Lebanon. Refusing to fight his fellow Arabs for an imperialist power, Qassim returns to Baghdad with his troops and opens fire on the royal palace.

The second floor of the palace, where the twenty-four-year-old king, Faisal II, is shaving in his underwear, catches fire. A young man without political interests, whose main passions are jazz and skiing, Faisal II remains from first to last dominated by the regent, Abd al-Illah. He tries to flee with his family, but the royal party is caught in the palace courtyard by Qassim's soldiers and machine-gunned to death. Faisal's body is wrapped in a carpet and buried secretly. From this time on, the building will be known as Qasr al-Nihayah, the Palace of the End, and will become a dread prison of torture and murder.

The regent is caught hiding behind a mirror. He is hurled from a palace window to the crowd below and his body is dragged through the streets. The only one to escape is the wily seventy-year-old royalist prime minister, Nuri al-Said. Having survived many a coup in the past, now he again uses his wits to disguise himself. He dresses as a veiled woman and flees to a Baghdad suburb. The next day, though, he will be recognized by a fruit vendor who follows him through the streets shouting his name. The old diplomat is caught by the crowd and impaled on a stake, his body left to satisfy the contempt of the passersby and the hunger of the street dogs.

The new ruler, General Qassim, immediately alienates the Baath Party and the army. He is more interested in creating a strong Iraqi state than in joining Nasser's pan-Arab union, and so he turns to the quickly growing Iraqi Communist Party for support, at the same time wooing Iraq's non-Arab ethnic groups such as the Kurds.

But his tactics will not prevail: he will be no more successful than the monarchy was at creating a patriotic national consciousness. Iraq is condemned to be drawn and quartered by opposing ethnic and religious forces. First there is the Shia, an extremist branch of Islam that makes up 55 percent of the population. Against them stand the orthodox Sunni Muslims, a minority, only 20 percent of the population, from which the ruling class is drawn. Then there are the non-Arab Kurds, who dream of a state of their own, a dream that is a nightmare for the secular Iraqi

Baathists, especially since 40 percent of Iraqi oil is in Kurdish territory. Adding to the chaos, these groups themselves break down into warring factions who oppose each other with as much bitterness as they do their mortal enemies. Finally, the bloodshed and strife are intensified by the fact that the large majority of Iraqis are used to only tribal authority and resist the idea of any central government.

All of this is too much for General Qassim, who has taken power but does not know how to wield it. His main achievement is, surprisingly enough, a charitable one: he is still remembered by the poor people for building thousands of small houses throughout Baghdad and the country. When later on he faces a firing squad, he will pathetically remind his executioners of his charity as he pleads for his life. In 1959, though, his demise is still four years away; the Baathist gunmen who wait for his car in the streets of Baghdad are premature. The young Saddam Hussein is among them, ordered by his party to help topple the pro-Communist leader for refusing to join Nasser's new order and for trying to suppress the Baathists.

It will be Saddam's second murder, but still he is nervous. A few months earlier, at his uncle Khairallah's instigation, Saddam made his bones by killing a member of the Takriti clan who chose communism over pan-Arabism. Afterward, Khairallah joined his nephew in jail, where the two drank and sang until dawn in celebration. A few days later, thanks to the political confusion of the times and with the help of Khairallah's Takriti army friends, they were both released and the investigation was dropped.

But now, as he stands on the streets of Baghdad with his fellow gunmen, it is not just some renegade clan member Saddam is hoping to murder, so perhaps his nervousness may be excused. Qassim is on his way to a meeting at the East German embassy, his car heading down al-Rashid Street, at that time a boulevard of elegant shops and open-air cafés. Saddam is supposed to provide cover for his fellow assassins but according to an official Iraqi propaganda version of events, "When Saddam found himself face to face with the dictator [General Qassim] he was unable to restrain himself. He forgot all his instructions and immediately opened fire."

If we look beneath the writer's intention, that is, to praise Saddam for his unrestrained fervor, we can place the blame for the failed assassination on Hussein. Qassim's driver and a bodyguard are instantly killed and the car, riddled with bullets, veers onto the street. The glass fronts of the facing jewelry stores and restaurant shatter and Qassim himself is seriously wounded. But Saddam's sudden impulse to step forward and shoot before his three partners have a chance to open fire enables Qassim's surviving bodyguards to recover and respond to the shock.

They commandeer a passing car, bundle the general into it, and, still shooting, get him to safety. In the confusion, Saddam and another of the assassins are wounded by their own fire as they flee. The incident is a deeply important one in Saddam's life. We see the psychic use he makes of it when, years later, he tells Jordan's King Hussein that he died there in the streets of Baghdad firing on General Qassim. After that he became a fatalist, he says; any years of life granted him are a gift. He fears no one and nothing.

Whatever his private feelings, the assassination attempt is certainly a turning point in his public career. Although he does not want to leave the country, now he must, and the time he spends in Egypt will be important in terms of his political education. If he does not complete high school in Cairo until he is twenty-four, he finds observing firsthand Nasser's methods of governing revolutionary Egypt more instructive.

The first step of that journey to Egypt begins after the assassination attempt and is made in disguise. Dressed in Bedouin robes, Saddam rides a horse out of Baghdad in the direction of his native village (a car from Baghdad would make him too conspicuous). He rides for four days, eating almost nothing, wounded in one leg—from which he himself cuts out a bullet—eluding the roadblocks and soldiers scouring the countryside for the assassins. Exhausted as he approaches his home, he tries to get a bargeman to ferry him across the Tigris at the village of Al-Dhouri, but the man refuses since it is late and there is a curfew. So Hussein abandons his horse and swims across the river, stumbling out of the cold water on the other shore with chattering teeth and soaking wet. A local villager puts him up for the night, and when the man gets suspicious the next morning, Hussein has only to mention his powerful clan to silence him. He has arrived on his home turf.

His family gets Saddam across the border to Syria, where he will spend three months in Damascus fraternizing with members of the Baath Party there and acquiring a valuable protector: Michel Aflaq, founder of the Party, a mystic, politician, and writer whose high opinion of Hussein will be a great asset over the years to come, legitimizing the peasant from Takrit. Logic and need dictate his next step, from Damascus to Cairo, since Nasser's government will financially support Baathist exiles from Iraq, the Egyptian president appreciating their opposition to Qassim.

Saddam will never be another Nasser: the fiery rhetoric of the Egyptian president rises to an almost visionary level while the passions he arouses in the crowd sweep all rational objections to one side. But Saddam watches the people's response to Nasser's day-by-day policies and will imitate him in his ability to substitute promise for reality, to describe defeat as triumph. When Saddam is later in control of Iraq he will imitate Nasser's use of a parliament to cloak one-party rule. And like Nasser, his politics will always sacrifice principle for power.★

In Egypt, Saddam spends much time in the Andiana Café, where he leaves behind unpaid bills and the memory of a brawl: getting into a political argument, he chases a fellow student through the streets of Cairo with a knife. After finally finishing high school he begins to study law at Cairo University, also on a stipend from Nasser's government. But he breaks off his studies to return to Baghdad in 1963, when the Baath Party succeeds in overthrowing General Qassim in a bloody coup. Hussein will complete his law degree in Iraq eight years later. Appearing for his exam at the University of Baghdad with four bodyguards, he will casually place a pistol on the desk in front of him, impressing his examiners accordingly.

Anyone watching TV in Baghdad in 1963 is witness to a strange spectacle. General Qassim has been executed by the Baathists, but still the rumor persists that he has escaped and will attempt a countercoup. To put an end to such hopes, the Baathists display the bloody corpse of the former leader on television, complete with close-ups of

---

★A good example is Nasser's response to Qassim's threat to take over Kuwait in 1961 (a foretaste of 1991). *Socialist, pan-Arabist* Nasser immediately teams up with *colonialist* Great Britain to save the *conservative* Gulf monarchy. Qassim's and Nasser's hatred of each other matters more to the Egyptian president than his pan-Arab ideals.

his lolling head. As an enthusiastic voice-over proclaims the virtues of the new socialist regime, a soldier grabs the dead man by the hair and spits in his face. Thus the party of Saddam Hussein comes to power.

A great wedding feast takes place soon after Saddam returns from Egypt. Khairallah Tulfah marries his daughter Sajida to his protégé with dancing and song and a joy heightened by the Baathist victory.

Amidst the noise and the drinking, a fortune-teller predicts good fortune and wealth for the family. Certainly the prediction will come true for Uncle Khairallah, his son, Adnan, and his daughter. When Saddam comes to power, his uncle is made mayor of Baghdad, and the old man amasses a fortune in real estate, buying up valuable properties for almost nothing; everyone knows what it means to refuse him. Adnan Khairallah will become minister of war; he is, after all, Saddam's boyhood friend and had stood by the young outcast when he first came to Takrit from al-Ouja. Sajida will become one of the richest women in the world. Her extravagance and greed will be legendary.

But if the Gypsy could have looked further into the future, she would have seen Sajida raging in her villa while Hussein makes love to his new wife. She would have seen Khairallah's son Adnan dying in a helicopter "accident," the kind of death that befalls those who criticize Hussein, boyhood friend or not. And she would have seen Uncle Khairallah at his son's funeral, lifting his arms to heaven and vowing eternal vengeance against the man—the boy—he taught to hate.

III.   JIHAZ HANEEN, THE INSTRUMENT OF YEARNING★

KARBALA, IRAQ, 1968. Black shapes move like shadows or figures in a frieze against the white walls of the ancient city. Overhead the noonday sun burns in the empty, Middle Eastern sky. The winding streets and narrow alleys are silent, but it is the silence of expectation.

Suddenly unearthly cries and piercing shrieks fill the air. A huge crowd of wailing women clad in black, their arms spread like great dark wings, surround ecstatic, chanting men. As the crowd moves forward, the men whip themselves with chains ending in knives or beat their bare heads with sticks until blood covers the dusty streets or stains the beautiful carpets laid out for the flagellants to walk on.

It is the hour the holy martyr Hussein was beheaded more than a thousand years before. But in this part of the world the past is never past. Year after year, generation after

---

★The internal security apparatus whose function it is to torture and kill the enemies of Saddam Hussein.

generation, on the tenth day of the Islamic month of Muharram the Shiites mourn their prophet as if he had just died that very moment. Ali and Hussein, the saints of the Shia branch of Islam, were born in Karbala and still "speak to" the nation from here. Masses of pilgrims from all over the world make their way to pray at the tombs in Najaf and Karbala in southern Iraq; there are 130 million adherents of Shia Islam.

In the Arab world, they are the dispossessed and the excluded, heretics ruled by the orthodox Sunnis. But persecution only intensifies their fervor. In contrast to the complacent oil-rich Sunni Arabs of Saudi Arabia or the Gulf sheikdoms, they are fanatics, eager to die for their faith. By the standards of the West, they are incomprehensible; while the young men of America and Europe dream of worldly success or great achievements or love, Shia's young men dream of martyrdom.

Although officially Iraq is a secular state, it is impossible to understand its political trauma without taking its Muslim roots into account. There are great Shiite slums in Baghdad and Basra, and the rural population in the south is largely Shiite as well; the salt marshes here have become places of refuge for them. During World War I, the British lost 23,000 men here. They are buried in a swamp a little below the level of the Tigris, with the tops of their gravestones just poking out of the slimy green water. Above the dead men, Shiite resistance fighters from Al Dawa el-Islamiyah, the Voice of Islam, crouch amidst the tall reeds while government helicopters circle overhead. They are resourceful and brave and scornful of death. Their strength stems from their faith, which began as and remains a faith of opposition.

Like the Sunnis, the Shiites accept the supremacy of the prophet Muhammad, an epileptic and visionary born into the Quraysh tribe of Mecca in A.D. 570. A driver of caravans crossing the desert (who married the rich widow he worked for), Muhammad heard a voice in the desert that called out to him, "Recite!" The archangel Gabriel thus transmitted chapter after chapter of what was to be the Koran. Over the next centuries, the voice of the desert will echo in the great civilized cities of the world as Baghdad and Damascus and finally Constantinople embrace the new faith.

Cleansing Mecca of idols is Muhammad's first task. He destroys the images which the pagans worshiped at the Kaaba, a huge black meteorite that becomes a central Muslim shrine. The new prophet proclaims the oneness of God and the supremacy of the Koran, to which all true believers must submit (*Muslim* means "the one who submits" in Arabic). The prophet's tastes, reflected in the new faith, are simple and ascetic, conforming to the harsh, nomadic life of the desert. And when Muhammad dies, his successor is chosen according to tribal law, on the basis of merit, not blood or wealth.

No difficulty arises over the succession in the early years of Islam. The "Rightly Guided Caliphs, the companions of the prophet," are universally respected. It is an era when the virtues of the nomads prevail in a democratic society, where the voices of wealth and privilege have not yet been raised. It is only with Uthmann, the fourth caliph (644–656), that strife begins. From the faith of simple tribesmen, Islam has become the banner of an empire. Conquering in the name of Allah, the caliphs are rich and powerful, prey to the temptations of the city.

Setting himself up as a rival to the "corrupt" or more worldly Uthmann, Muhammad's son-in-law Ali claims leadership for himself. Ali represents the poorer families of Mecca and those who originally studied at Muhammad's feet; his goal is to return to what he perceives as the true faith. The caliph Uthmann is murdered, but his death only widens the growing rift in Islam. Aishah, the prophet's favorite wife, hates the reformer Ali and accuses him of cowardice for refusing to punish those who killed Uthmann. From a litter on the back of a camel, Aishah leads Bedouin fighters against Ali, who is victorious in what is known as the Battle of the Camel in Shiite hagiography. But the victory is a hollow one. In 661 Ali is assassinated before he can found an Islamic empire according to his precepts. With his last breath, the martyr requests to be buried wherever his camel kneels. His tomb thus becomes the holy Shiite shrine at Najaf in Iraq.

Ali's second son, Hussein, grandson of the prophet, also dies a martyr to the faith, a sword in one hand, the Koran in the other. Like his father, he is ambushed and slaughtered along with supporters; their death at the hands of the worldly and corrupt is glorified in Shiite dogma. Shia is a faith of suffering, betrayal, martyrdom, and salvation. Hussein's great shrine in Karbala and Ali's tomb at Najaf are the two most sacred places in Shia, memorials to those who fight against great odds for a pure and uncompromising vision.

Against this ancient religious force is counterpoised in the 1960s the secular philosophy of the socialist Baath Party, no less fierce, and determined to rule over the Shiite majority. The first Baathist coup of 1963, which brings Saddam Hussein back from Egypt, is bloody and violent beyond measure, although the Baathists will lose their grip on power after a mere nine months.

When a Shiite coup displaces the Baath Party, evidence of Baathist cruelty is uncovered in the cellars of the Palace of the End. A British observer notes "electric wires with pincers, pointed iron stakes on which prisoners were made to sit, and a machine which still bore traces of chopped-off fingers. Small heaps of bloodied clothing were scattered about, and there were pools of blood on the floor and stains over the wall."

The first Baath grab at power fails not because the Party is unwilling to exercise the extremes of repression; its stumbling block instead is the intraparty divisions and purges that leave its leadership in shambles. The new, Shiite, president of Iraq dies after a short term in power and is replaced by his brother, Abd al-Rahman Aref; both are insignificant figures on the political scene, men without a strong vision, who try to preserve an unsatisfactory status quo. Members of the Baath Party, Saddam among them, go underground. After a period in hiding, however, Saddam is captured by the anti-Baathist regime in a twelve-hour shoot-out that ends only when he uses up all of his ammunition. He will spend two years in prison with his colleagues, finally escaping and going into hiding again to help plot Baath's return to power.

With Israel's triumph in the 1967 war, the crowds riot and even the non-Baathist army officers have had enough of the weak and indecisive leadership. The second Baathist coup in '68 is bloodless. Saddam's cousin, the senior army officer Ahmed Hassan al-Bakr, places him in charge of the security apparatus in the new government. In the decade starting with the overthrow of the monarchy in 1958, Iraq has known four successful coups and countless attempted coups, with sporadic massacres and riots in between. But now the coupling of Bakr's prestige and Saddam's violence and vigilance will provide the Baath with a leadership that promises stability in Iraq.

The price of this stability is another matter. Thousands upon thousands of Communists, leftists, Shiites and Kurds are arrested and tortured, some on the mere suspicion of hostility to the new regime. Iraqi Jews are targeted as "Zionist spies" and hanged after being dragged through frenzied crowds in torchlit processions. Trials of former government members are conducted as ghoulish spectacles, with illiterate peasants streaming in from the country to watch broken and tortured "criminals" confess their guilt.

Advancement in the so-called Security Division depends on how far an officer is willing to give himself up to savagery. One of Hussein's most trusted subordinates, Nadhim Khazr, achieves his position because of his skill at "interrogation," a skill which consists of nothing more than extinguishing lighted cigarettes on his victims' eyeballs. (Khazr eventually ends up before a firing squad himself in 1973 for turning on Hussein and his cousin.)

There is a photo from this time of Saddam with a needle and thread next to a pretty ten-year-old girl; he is mending the lace sleeve of his daughter's party dress. Other photos show Saddam with his young son Uday at the beach, or Saddam teaching Uday how to hunt near the lakes of al-Habbaniya. There is a simple, fatherly joy in his expression. It is impossible to detect any sign that he is master of the Jihaz Haneen, the Instrument of Yearning, a force so ruthless that it will enslave the Iraqi people for the next thirty years.

By 1979 Saddam has come into his own. He no longer needs his military cousin, al-Bakr. Intimidated by the enormous power of Saddam's Secret Police, his relative docilely steps down from the leadership and leaves Saddam alone in the spotlight.

During the next decade, the '80s, death will stalk through Iraq with such intensity that the horrors of the

'70s—foremost among them, perhaps, the indiscriminate slaughter and mass deportation of 300,000 Kurds—will be almost forgotten.

In 1979 revolution topples the Shah of Iran. Convinced that his neighbor is weak and in disarray, Hussein goes on the attack, incited by sycophants, who must appear warlike to stay in favor. His lackeys assure him the war will last a month, no longer. That "month," however, will stretch into eight years and claim millions of lives. It will be the bloodiest battle the Middle East has ever known.

IV.   THE KEYS TO HEAVEN

**I lie awake at night worrying about those terrible
biological weapons.**
　　　　　　　　　—King Fahd of Saudi Arabia

WAR WITH IRAN. Two revealing scenes:

The first, a field outside of Khorramshar, Iran, May
1982. This major Iranian city had fallen to Iraq a year earlier, in the first months of the war. In the confusion and
disorder after the revolution, the Iranians were unprepared
for Saddam's onslaught. But now Khomeini sends his answer.

Groups of Iranian youths approach the field from three
directions. They are handcuffed together should one of
them suddenly be seized by panic and try to flee. At a signal, they walk forward slowly, deliberately, their faces shining with ecstasy. Around their necks are wooden keys,
which have been distributed by an Iranian officer of the
Revolutionary Guard. Designed by the Ayatollah Khomeini, the keys are pledges that *when* the youths die (not *if*),
they will be rewarded with the bliss of heaven.

Lacking mine sweepers, the Ayatollah clears the fields

with these teenagers so that no harm will come to the precious tanks that follow. One by one they are blown to bits,
shouting praises to God for granting them glory. Their
mothers and fathers will scrawl their names on the Wall of
Martyrs. Their sweethearts will mourn them near
Teheran's Fountain of Blood. And their brothers, too
young to join them, will visit the vast graveyards around
the capital, sick with envy that they have not yet been
chosen to die.

The second scene from the war takes place in Iraq, on
the outskirts of Basra, in 1982. By this stage in the war, the
Iraqis have been thrust off Iranian soil while the Iranian
army has advanced to within artillery range of this capital
of the south. Heavy fighting is within earshot as Saddam
arrives with Uday. He orders his son to attack the Iranians.
In a melodramatic voice, a general begs the president not
to send Uday on this perilous mission. But Uday ignores
him, taking off in a helicopter, from which he can be seen
firing missiles (later it turns out that *Iraqi* troops were hit).
But the whole event is staged propaganda, a trick for the
press and photographers.

The scenes sum up the inner emotional truth of the
war. For Saddam, the conflict is an opportunity. The Iranian revolution gives him a chance to seize land and pre-
eminence in the Gulf, so he drags his brutalized nation
into the ill-fated adventure.

For the Iranians, members of the Shia sect, the war is
a crusade against the Unbeliever. Attacked, they unite behind Khomeini, their Shiite prophet.

Saddam presents the conflict as one of the Arab nation
versus the non-Arab Persians, trying to minimize the Ayatollah's appeal to Iraq's Arab-Shiite masses.

Khomeini calls for revolution not only among Iraq's
dispossessed Shiites, but among the poor Shiite workers in

the Gulf sheikdoms as well, calling for the whole Arab world to throw off its corrupt and secular rulers.

And so it goes, with elements of culture, religion, and nationality all playing their parts, the web of allegiances becoming ever more tangled and difficult to follow, with only one guiding principle a constant: *The enemy of my enemy is my friend.* Baathist Arab Syria, for example, will side against Baathist Arab Iraq and with non-Arab Iran. That is, a secular Arab state comes to the aid of a fundamentalist non-Arab state, since Syria's Assad and Iraq's Saddam are at daggers drawn over national disputes. Similarly, at Saddam's lowest point in the war, he will actually turn to his enemy's enemy, Israel, seeking military help, which Israel refuses. The war proves the hollowness of all ideological pretenses, the uncertainty of every identity.

If a single symbol had to be found to sum up the futility of the war, it is the Shatt al-Arab, the "River of the Arabs," "the prize," a maritime route inland from the Gulf which both Iran and Iraq claim. It is because of the waterway that the Shah of Iran, in the 1970s, sends money and arms to the Kurds to weaken Iraq, forcing Saddam to abandon his claim to it.★

In 1980, Saddam tears up his agreement with Iran as his first act of war, attacking Iran across the Shatt al-Arab. And at the end of the war, Saddam claims victory despite the millions of deaths, because he gains no more, no less, than

---

★It is one of the ironies of history that in the 1970s Saddam gives refuge to Khomeini, the Ayatollah being the enemy of Saddam's enemy the Shah. Khomeini will live for six years in Iraq's holy Shiite cities before leaving for France, from which country he will return to topple the Shah in 1979.

the waterway. (To be lost again, incredibly, almost comically, in the war over Kuwait, when Saddam buys Iranian neutrality—by giving up his right to the coveted waterway.)

Part of this obsession stems from the fact that "Geography is Iraq's enemy," as Saddam muses at the beginning of the war. The cards nature has dealt Saddam give him a difficult hand to play, since all the aces, all the strategic advantages, are Iran's. Baghdad, for example, is only seventy miles from the Iranian border and Basra is only thirteen, making both crucial cities vulnerable to Iranian attack, while the vast landmass of Iran provides it with strategic depth and cover. Then too Iran has more than thirteen-hundred miles of coast from which to ship its oil, while Iraq is almost landlocked, with a scrap of coast twenty miles long and a pipeline running through enemy soil. Syria will shut Iraq's pipeline during the war, costing Saddam $30 million a day.

And so on and on; the list of Iran's natural advantages is a long one, which Saddam can only counter with an *unnatural* one of his own: chemical weapons, mustard gas and cyanide and VX nerve agent, a harvest of scientific death purchased with Iraqi oil. Chemical weapons, or the threat of them, will prove decisive. After eight years of inconclusive struggle, with wave after wave of fanatical Iranian martyrs breaking over the Iraqi troops, after the war of the cities, and the war of the boats, the holy wars waged in the mosques and the financial wars waged in the banks, Saddam prepares a final nightmare for Teheran: missiles with huge poison warheads, accompanied by shattering-glass bombs to make sure the destruction is massive.

Word spreads of Saddam's intention. The aged Ayatollah is interrupted at his prayers. And finally, though

Khomeini has vowed not to relent until Saddam is toppled from power, even he is shaken by the cruelty of the plan. Khomeini allows negotiations with Iraq to begin.

In the wild joy of this Pyrrhic victory, Saddam turns to the ancient warriors of his land for a source of identification and national pride. He rebuilds the tombs of the rulers of Mesopotamia (a Greek name meaning "the land between the rivers," the Tigris and the Euphrates). Millions of bricks are baked with the inscription "The Babylon of Nebuchadnezzar was reconstructed in the era of Saddam Hussein," a fitting role model, since Nebuchadnezzar was the king who enslaved both the Jews and the Persians.

At a victory bash, laser beams project Saddam's features in the sky, superimposed on those of the Babylonian tyrant. The resemblance is uncanny, the applause unrestrained.

A fantastic triumphal arch is erected in Baghdad. Two metal forearms, their shape taken from a cast of Saddam's own arms, each forty feet long, reach out of the ground holding steel sabers whose tips cross. The Iraqi army parades under this arch, dragging a net filled with the helmets of dead Iranians.

For all the celebration, though, there is a dreadful, iron logic which will soon bring the Iraqis back to reality. The end of the war with Iran almost inevitably results in the next war, with Kuwait. And Iraq's million-man army will now return home to a life of severe privation. From a wealthy country with $30 billion in oil reserves, Iraq has debts in the neighborhood of $70 billion, most of which will never be repaid.

The soldiers have lived with daily violence for eight

years, and the scenes of carnage cannot suddenly be forgotten on their return to civilian life.

The returned soldiers vent their blood lust on the foreign workers. But the first symptom of national sickness is kept wrapped in mystery. Thousands of coffins containing the bodies of Egyptian foreign workers are shipped from Iraq back to Cairo without explanation. Riots and unrest shake the Kurdish north and the Shiite south and are put down with brutal force.

Addressing the nation, Saddam channels the people's discontent. What have the Saudis and rich Gulf sheiks contributed besides money? he asks. And what is money next to the suffering the Iraqis have endured? Demanding billions from Kuwait and Saudi Arabia to rebuild his ruined country, Saddam asks, where would his neighbors be if fanatical Iran had won? A master of propaganda and rhetoric, as always he knows how to play to the crowd, conjuring billionaire emirs and penniless Iraqi soldiers without the money to buy prosthetic arms and legs.

And so the cycle continues, an endless repetition of violence and repression plays itself out. Kuwait and its aftermath are variations on a theme Saddam has already performed a hundred times over. The players remain the same, the Shiites, the Kurds, the Sunnis, the Baathists; familiar too are the tactics, the goals, the greed, the power of hate.

But always there is some embellishment, some new phrase or cynical idea to suit the moment. When American troops arrive to protect Saudi Arabia, for example, Saddam has the word spread that female Jewish soldiers are desecrating Mecca by tossing rags soaked in menstrual blood on the Kaaba, the great shrine. When UN teams arrive to search for chemical weapons, he has weeping Iraqi mothers hand the foreigners the corpses of dead babies, infants killed by UN sanctions. Fiendish and primitive, Saddam searches for atavistic images that will outrage and sicken, cunningly directing the despair of the defeated.

THE FINAL QUESTION

THE YEAR 1356, TAKRIT. Tamerlane with his Mongol horde stops to destroy this obscure village-fortress on his way to Baghdad. Annihilating the desert warriors who try to defend it, he leaves behind a pyramid of human skulls to mark the occasion.

Takrit, six-hundred years later. Saddam Hussein plays his first childish games in the ruined fortress—in the shadow of Tamerlane's pyramid. As a man, he will build his own monuments to cruelty and horror: the Qasr al-Nihayah, the Palace of the End; the Kurds murdered with chemical weapons; the senseless eight-year war with Iran; the rape of Kuwait; the massacres of Shiites in Narjaf and Karbala and the desecration of their shrines. They are towering monuments indeed, worthy of Tamerlane. The question that remains, one that Saddam must sometimes ask himself in the quiet hours of the night, is will the last skull in the pyramid be his own?

AFTERWORD

OF BLOOD AND SPLENDOR

When Idi Amin ruled Uganda, the alligators were observed to grow lazy and lethargic: he threw so many bodies into the rivers that they were surfeited with human flesh. The bastard son of a witch doctor mother, Amin was raised in poverty and subjected to humiliation, watching his mother sell her body to soldiers during his boyhood in the impoverished no-man's land near the Sudan-Uganda border. After becoming "President for Life," Amin himself resorted to sorcery, murdering his favorite son, a ten-year-old named Moise, and eating his heart in a ritual supposed to bring him good luck. At the same time, Amin negotiated trade agreements with Great Britain, attended conferences on African unity, and dealt with the International Monetary Fund as if he were not a psychopath.

This madness-within-sanity, this ability to deal with objective reality while remaining preoccupied by ghastly obsessions, is characteristic of all tyrants to one degree or another. When Churchill described Hitler as a madman to Stalin during the Second World War, Stalin shook his head ruefully, commenting, "He would never have gotten so far if he were mad." Stalin was in a position to know. The madness that propels these men to power is mixed in good measure with the leaven of cunning, even, occasionally, genius. There is an equation, a balance between sanity and mania, which must be maintained if the tyrant is to endure; and if this equation is upset, the tyrant's days are numbered.

But such seeming rationality only makes the tyrant all the more dangerous; for beneath the calm exterior lurks murderous, psychopathic impulses which are acted on suddenly, without cause and without warning. Hussein, for example, while addressing his National Assembly, notices a delegate passing a note to a colleague and shoots him for conspiracy on the spot, resuming his speech after acknowledging the terrified and awed applause.

What does it mean, though, to call him a psychopath? It is a deceptively safe category, which distances his behavior from our own: he is sick and we are well; he is brutal and we are normal. But it must be remembered that such distinctions are ones of degree, not kind. We may have control over our aggressive or narcissistic impulses while an Amin or a Hitler may not, but we are on the same human continuum.

Freud's great contribution was to teach us the relevance of that which we call sick, aberrant, pathological, stating with intellectual bravery at the beginning of his career, "Nothing which is human is foreign to me." The depth of the human mind reveals itself in extremes. And what we learn by dwelling on the monstrous and the atavistic teaches us much about ourselves that we would like to forget.*

---

*As an interesting aside, it may be noted that Freud's famous credo, definitive of modern thought, was taken from a quip in a bawdy Roman comedy, the answer an unlucky son gives his father when the two accidentally meet in a whorehouse.

As John Huston observes in the movie *Chinatown,* "What you have to realize is that most people, under the right circumstances, are capable of *anything.*" And what Huston says of individuals applies to whole societies as well. "An oppressed people always deserves its fate," the Marquis de Custine reflects in the early 1800s after visiting tsarist Russia. "Tyranny is achieved by a whole nation. It is not the accomplishment of a single individual."

That is, tyrants have not only been tolerated but *embraced* in political experience. The tyrant must be something like a medium or a national oracle who experiences the deepest fears and desires of his people and gives voice to them. It is not merely a question of dominating a nation by brute force, but of being in touch with its unconscious or secret wishes.

We are talking about "success stories" in this book: Nero was sincerely mourned by the masses of the Roman world. Ivan held Russia in his power for more than forty years (causing terror by simply threatening to abdicate!). Hitler commanded the loyalty of his people for twelve years. Stalin died in power after thirty years of playing demigod to 200 million people. Saddam Hussein has been in power for thirty years in a nation previously racked by political instability. None of them, however, would have been successful in a different place or at a different time.

One key element in the unholy marriage between tyrant and nation is "the enemy." It is no accident that each of these tyrants stirred up his people's rage and loathing against a people from whom they thought they needed protection. For Nero it was the Christians; for Ivan, the old Russian nobility; for Hitler, the Jews; for Stalin, the saboteurs of the revolution; for Saddam Hussein, the imperialist West. The list is endless—for Pol Pot, the intellectuals; for Amin, the Asians; and so on and on.

Another key factor is charisma, as important to a tyrant as it is to a prophet or a movie star. To return for a moment to Amin, "His excellency, Field Marshal, Lord of all the Beasts of the Earth and Fishes of the Sea and Conqueror of the British Empire in Africa in General and Uganda in Particular," as he modestly called himself in official documents. He is a man filled with murderous rage, who took in with his mother's milk the resentments and hatreds of rural, tribal Uganda. And yet he is also lusty, charming, ironic, and physically strong, a heavyweight boxing champion in Uganda's colonial days. His "jokes" are repeated up and down the land. When the president of neighboring Tanzania criticizes his policies, he mockingly feigns hurt feelings and says that he, Amin, loves the president so much that if the Tanzanian were a woman he would marry him despite his gray hair. He telegrams Nixon his congratulations during Watergate. And sometimes there is an element of high seriousness in his jokes, of what Schlegel would call transcendental buffoonery, as when he enters the Organization of African Unity conference in a litter carried by six white men to symbolize the new "white man's burden."

Amin's case ended with him being forced to flee to Saudi Arabia, where, suffering from venereal disease, he spent his days in prayer. But if Amin falters, other tyrants are sustained to the end by their charismatic appeal despite the tragedy and suffering they create. After the Kuwaiti debacle, Hussein transforms Iraqi misery into a source of patriotic pride. Although the country is in ruins, he celebrates with parades and speeches and rallies: he and his people have achieved victory in successfully defying the West. His use of human shields, his deliberate pollution of the air with burning oil wells and of the seas with massive oil slicks were a shock to our Western consciousness. But he was playing to his people, not us, and realized the need for spectacle during a crisis that could have brought him down.

Thus spectacle, display, splendor, is interwoven with the tyrant's personal charisma in such regimes. On his first visit to Italy, in 1934, Hitler was dressed in a yellow raincoat and striped trousers, with patent leather shoes. The Italians enjoyed a good laugh at his expense. Mussolini, on the other hand, wore a magnificent uniform of his own design, with a ceremonial dagger at his side, black boots, and silver spurs. Hitler, mortified, would never make the same mistake.

Such flamboyance was typical of Mussolini even before he swaggered onto the world stage. Taking the exam to become an elementary school teacher, he showed up in black clothes, typical of the anarchists, complete with dangling cigarette. And working as a famous journalist for the right wing *Il Popolo d'Italia,* he used a hand grenade for a paper weight. The *style* of Italian fascism was so significant that it determined its content, reinforcing Mussolini's propaganda that he was the glory of the ancient Romans come to life. And the relationship between the two was something that Mussolini never forgot.

Part of the charisma of these leaders stems from the fact that they indulge in behavior which at once fascinates and repels. "The bliss of murder, the joy of shedding another's blood," one of Kafka's characters rhapsodizes; and truly, the tyrant achieves power by breaking a primal taboo with his arbitrary use of brute force. If nature is hierarchical, with the strongest predator at the top of the feeding chain, then to the degree that humankind is a part of nature, violence and aggression must appeal to us as the call of the wild.

But while we are the children of nature, we are also something more—or perhaps less, depending on the point of view. Aristotle calls man a political animal. For the philosopher, the word "political" is still close to its Greek root "polis," meaning city. And to create that "polis," to create human society, we have to give up our indiscriminate aggression. Two thousand years later, however, Dostoyevsky was still able to distinguish human beings from their fellow animals not because they are political, but because "man is the only animal who can curse." Civilization hasn't banished cruelty, it has only refined it. And indeed his definition has resonance in the face of our tyrants' excessive and, thus, unnatural, cruelty.

Their endless murders and tortures are certainly beyond what is necessary for survival. Their fears bear little in common with reality. Their cruelty is not about "the survival of the fittest," to paraphrase the words of the naturalist Darwin, but bears out Nietzsche's axiom, "the survival of the [morally] unfittest."

Even the parental instincts of our tyrants are warped, as witnessed by Amin's cannibalistic murder of his son. While it is true that certain animals devour their young, this is not the norm in nature. Yet of the tyrants discussed in this book, three kill their children: Nero kicks his pregnant wife to death; Ivan the Terrible beats his son to death; and Stalin refuses to help his son when he is captured by the Nazis. Saddam Hussein raises up a monster in his own image, whom he is only prevented from killing by the hysterical pleas of his wife. Hitler can have no sons at all, because he can find sexual satisfaction only in extreme acts of masochism.

The sickness of these tyrants is central to their power. If part of our fascination with psychopaths like the fictional Hannibal Lecter is their ability to be both brilliant and insane at the same time, Ivan the Terrible or Hitler may be said to go one step further. Playing to the worst, most atavistic impulses of their nations, they make their aberrant obsessions central, normative.

In this respect, Tokugawa Tsunayoshi's long despotic reign is definitive of the godlike power of the tyrant. He would become known as the "Dog Shogun" because of his concern for the welfare of all animals, from fish to falcons to mosquitoes, but during his thirty years of rule, from 1680 to 1709, he would become known for an equally intense contempt for his Japanese subjects. The innumerable decrees he passed in a manifesto entitled *The Laws of Compassion for Living Things* read like fantasy. A network of spies covered the land, condemning thousands for absurdities such as not addressing a dog respectfully: "Honorable Mr. Dog."

Toward the end of his reign, Tsunayoshi's caprices darken into cruel madness. The guilty are crucified for wounding an animal or beheaded for not stopping a dog fight. Prisoners who die in jail awaiting their trials are not spared: their corpses are pickled so that they might be brought before the judge to receive sentence. Outside Edo (Tokyo), shelters are established for more than fifty-thousand abandoned dogs, whose food and care are paid for by oppressive taxes even during a time of famine. While we may laugh at the absurdity of such a situation, as the great playwright Chikamatsu does in his seventeenth-century satire, still our laughter must be tempered by the knowledge of how much human suffering was involved.

Tsunayoshi's radical program is based on his idiosyncratic interpretation of Buddhism and of Confucian ethics, of which he was a serious if flawed student. And for all the strangeness of his laws, they are typical of an element in every tyrannical regime: the promise of revolutionary change, the exaltation of some ideal or dogma or doctrine in the name of which the tyranny demands life-or-death obedience.

Perhaps the most shocking of these cruel regimes was the one instituted by the Cambodian tyrant, Pol Pot. After his years of guerrilla warfare in the jungles and mountains, Pol Pot declares 1975 the first year of a new era, literally the year zero on the official calendar. Pol Pot's Khmer Rouge finally enter the capital, Phnom Penh, and order the entire population out into the countryside to dig ditches and plant rice, in forced labor that lasts from morning to night. The sick, the old, those unable to endure the harsh regimen are killed on the oft-repeated principle "To keep you alive is no gain to us; to kill you is no loss."

The use of money is forbidden. Owning books or wearing glasses, the sign of the intellectual, is enough to condemn a person to death. Ethnic minorities are slaughtered. Boy-soldiers shoot whomever they please. Ignorance is glorified. Cambodia is ruled by "Brother Number One" or "The High Organization"—nobody knows who. The name "Pol Pot" is a non-name, the Cambodian version of "John Doe," a pseudonym the mysterious leader has picked out because it is so common. Only after he is in power for a year, do U.S. analysts finally put together a piece of the puzzle: Pol Pot was born Saloth Sar. But who is this Saloth Sar?

Truly, he is a dark mystery. The few facts we know about him raise more questions than they answer. Everything he does, he does secretly; and for years at a time, nothing at all is known of his life. Unlike Hitler, Stalin, or Mussolini, who develop cults of personality, Pol Pot is terror without a face.

If we are to draw the most characteristic picture of him, a picture that does not change for more than thirty years, it would be this one: his small, delicate hands ply a fan as he goes on and on in his soft, musical voice, expounding, theorizing, elaborating. Whether he is hiding in a guerrilla camp or ruling from the ghostly capital he has created, his chief relationship to his followers is that of an inspired teacher to his pupils.

The ideals he preaches never change, from the time he is a student until long after the disaster of his rule. His goals have been formed by the examples of Mao's cultural revolution and Stalin's collectives and, ironically enough, they also owe much to the Cambodian Buddhist doctrines of self-renunciation, right action, and self-transformation, as interpreted by him, of course. Life, reality, facts, the suffering of a nation teach him nothing.

Time and experience do not dim Pol Pot's visionary fervor, a fervor which produces the "bureaucracy of death," the horrors of the Tuol Sleng prison, the absurdities of his Four-Year Plan, and the war with Vietnam, making Cambodia one of the worst disasters in the post–World War II world, with more than two million of its citizens senselessly slaughtered for a revolutionary "ideal" that can never be realized.

Similarly, the young Robespierre, learning to make lace at his grandmama's knee as he studies Latin, is a lion cub sharpening his claws. His intellect, when fully developed, will send thousands to the guillotine, that first attempt at efficiency and impersonality in slaughter. This "Archangel of Terror" will cast his shadow over the French Revolution. His death mask reveals more about the man than his volume of speeches: the proud, intellectual, pockmarked features, the lips compressed as if they would speak—yet one more oration!—the brow contracted in thought. Robespierre's violence is *intellectual* violence, the cruelty of thought, which we will later encounter with Lenin.

For all the variety in the rogues' gallery we have considered, there is the dull monotony of pornography in the spectacle of death and suffering necessary in a tyrannical society. Yet from Nero's massacre of the Christians to Stalin's great purges, the populace is awed and spellbound at the sight. In his essay *On the Sublime and Beautiful,* Edmund Burke observes, "Represent the most sublime and affecting tragedy we have . . . and when you have collected your audience, just at the moment when their minds are filled with expectation, let it be reported that a criminal is on the point of being executed in the adjoining square. . . . And in a moment, the theater will be empty."

In bloody rituals of execution and repression, the leader becomes the ancient god-king stepping forward to save his people, a promise as dangerous as it is seductive. If there is one lesson we can take away from the extravagant lives of our tyrants, it is the fragility of our democratic society, which, after all, is the exception not the norm in the dark, violent story known as human history.

INDEX